THE SPICE STORE

Choosing and using herbs and spices—the natural way to delicious food

For the past twenty years Bart Spices have produced a growing range of spices, herbs and seasonings, and now offer a range of 80 varieties, each of the finest quality.

I am sure our customers will have noticed Bart Spices don't just 'follow the field' – just a glance through our Gourmet Spice Jars, Double Value Packs and Good Cook Drums will reveal some of the more unusual and exotic spices like cardamoms, Chinese five spice, curry leaves, green pepper berries, Jamaican pepper, Sichuan pepper and so many more.

Then, take a look at the way we package our spices. We don't use plastic drums or jars with push-on or screw-top lids for any nose to enquire into. All our jars and drums have FreshSeal closures, which means the product is properly sealed, its qualities retained and you, the purchaser, are the only one to open it.

We at Bart Spices try to offer our customers the very best – in product, in packaging and in price.

One last point, we don't use any additives, artificial colouring, or preservatives, except a free-flowing ingredient such as calcium stearate in our salt-based products like garlic and onion salt.

So, remember, it's Bart Spices 'Naturally'.

R.J. Bartlam,
Managing Director

THE SPICE STORE

Choosing and using herbs and spices—the natural way to delicious food

with Bart Spices

THORSONS PUBLISHING GROUP

First published 1989

© BART SPICES 1989

British Library Cataloguing in Publication Data

The spice store: choosing and using herbs
and spices – the natural way to delicious food
1. Spices   2. Culinary herbs
641.3'383

ISBN 0-7225-1983-4

*Published by Thorsons Publishers Limited, Wellingborough, Northamptonshire,
NN8 2RQ, England*

Typeset by Book Ens, Saffron Walden, Essex
Printed in Great Britain by Richard Clay, Bungay, Suffolk

1   3   5   7   9   10   8   6   4   2

CONTENTS

Introduction 7
Part 1 – About herbs and spices 9
Some origins, history and uses of spices and herbs 9
Herbs and spices: what's the difference? 13
What is the best way to store spices? 14
How to cook with herbs and spices 16
Preservation of herbs and spices 18
The range of herbs and spices 20
Bart Spices' seasonings and blends 35
Quick cooking guide 39
Part 2 – Recipes using herbs and spices 47
Starters and salads 47
Light meals 52
Main courses 57
Puddings and desserts 82
Biscuits and bread 84
Sauces, dressings and stuffings 87
A barbecue party 92
Index 95

INTRODUCTION

'Off at sea north-east winds blow Sabian odours from the spicy shore of Araby, the blessed.'

Milton's *Paradise Lost.*

It is said the sense of smell can evoke a memory or trigger the imagination more than any other stimulus. Who has not, on detecting the aroma of garlic, been instantly transported to the Mediterranean with its olive trees, sunshine and vineyards?

Cooking with spices opens a portal to a new culinary world; the delicacy of China, the fire of Mexico, the richness of India and the colour of Malaysia and the Spice Islands.

We live in an age of bland convenience and stereotyped foods. This has brought with it a need to enrich and enliven. With the meeting of different cultures through cheap travel and the increased immigration of other nationalities into Britain, the range of tastes and flavours available to the general public has widened considerably.

The process of change, however, is a slow one. Although there can be few people in Britain today who have not yet experienced dining in an Indian, Chinese or Italian restaurant, most would not have the confidence to experiment with these types of cuisine in their own homes. This is unfortunate, for in most cases the addition of a spice or two may transform an otherwise common dish into something more exotic, or plain cooking into *haute cuisine.* What is Chilli con Carne, after all, but the humble minced beef and onions with the magic ingredient of chilli powder?

In this book we attempt to illustrate how easy it is to create exciting and exotic dishes, and we explain about the herbs and spices available, suggesting ways they can be used.

It is most important, however, to experiment. Recipes are really only guidelines, but spices should be used on a day-to-day basis to improve *every* dish. Far too many people display their spice rack as a 'Kitchen Rembrandt', only admiring its looks but failing to make full use of its contents. We hope you will discover there are few foods not improved by the use of herbs and spices.

Bon appetit!

PART I: ABOUT HERBS AND SPICES

SOME ORIGINS, HISTORY AND USES OF SPICES AND HERBS

Although spices are now of less importance as an article of trade than in former times, there is still a great demand for them in both Eastern and Western countries. Most spices are of tropical, Asian origin and because of the ever increasing population in these regions the local demand remains high. In the western world the nature of the demand has altered over the years and whilst better methods of preserving food have lessened the need of spices for this purpose, the canning industry and food manufacturers in general have discovered many new uses for them.

For many thousands of years the small curls of bark, dried leaves, dried roots and shrivelled berries have travelled along the winding trade routes of antiquity into legend and history.

Centuries before Christ, in about 1727 BC, there is a reference in the Old Testament to Joseph being sold by his brothers to Ishmaelite merchants who were bringing spice from India into Egypt. The route they travelled was from India by boat to the Gulf of Arabia and then by camel to Casson, on the Mediterranean coast. These Arab merchants of over 3000 years ago had a virtual monopoly of the spice trade from India. The Chinese and the Javanese brought spices grown in their countries as far as India where the Arab merchants traded for them; therefore their monopoly extended to nearly all spice growing areas of the world at that time. For centuries they would not disclose the secrets of their sources of supply but carried on their exceedingly profitable trade into the waiting markets of Carthage, Alexandria and Rome. Their only competition came from the Phoenicians who, being excellent seafarers, carried spices by sea into the port of Tyre. At the beginning of the Christian era other seafarers discovered how to make full use of the monsoon winds in the Indian Ocean that blow to the east in the summer and the west in the winter, thus enabling them to reach such markets as Rome in record time.

In about 800 AD new routes were opened and spices came via the river Indus and the river Oxus, then across the Caspian Sea, up the Volga and down to the sea of Azov. Trade during this period was very much influenced by the rise of the new religion Islam and the followers of Mohammed spread his word through Asia and the Middle East. As they travelled they gathered and traded in spices and spread knowledge of their uses along with their culture. When the Moors landed in Spain in 700 AD they brought this trade and knowledge with them.

By this time there was considerable rivalry for trade between Alexandria and Constantinople. From Egypt spices were taken via Italian ports over the Alps to the great trading centres at Bruges, this being the headquarters of the Hanseatic League and which had branches in London to the west, Novogorod in the east and Stockholm in the north. The Sultan of Egypt decided to derive personal gain from the trade and taxed all spices entering Egypt. This put up the price of spices in Europe considerably. Pepper was almost priceless; it was used to pay taxes, dowries, rents and was counted berry by berry; and still the Europeans did not know the source of all this wealth.

In 1271 a family of Venetian merchants set out for Cathay and the Far East, a voyage which lasted 24 years, during which time they explored all the territories of the East and China, and as a result of which Marco Polo wrote his eye-witness account of the journey. Inspired by the story, a young Genoese sea captain set out to find India and decided to do this by sailing westward—and thus Columbus discovered America.

From the early 15th century the successive Kings of Portugal had financed various expeditions in search of the source of spices with such famous navigators as Magellan, Diaz and, later in the century, Vasco de Gama. De Gama's expedition of 1497 was particularly successful in reaching Callicut in India where they traded in spices, gold and cloths, and made many friends. Leaving on the

20 November 1498 they reached Lisbon on the 18 September 1499. This was a great saving in time as spices brought through Egypt and Italy took 2 years to arrive.

In the year 1502 Portugal and Spain made an agreement. Portugal was to have the eastern trade and Spain the western trade. In 1509 no spices left Ceylon, Sumatra, Borneo, Java or the Moluccas without the knowledge of the Portuguese and by 1515 they were regarded as rulers of the Indian Ocean. This caused great concern to Egypt and Italy who saw their trade dwindling.

In 1579 the Netherlands declared their independence. Both Spain and Portugal forbade their subjects to trade with Holland, and, not being able to obtain spices from Madrid and London, the Dutch decided to go out to India themselves. This they did successfully taking control of Malacca, the Malay peninsula and northern Sumatra. By 1658 they controlled the cinnamon trade of Ceylon and by 1663 the rich pepper ports on the Malabar coast, Java and Celibes. They therefore took over the position formerly held by Portugal as 'Lords of the sea'.

Meanwhile, in England, as far back as the 12th century, a Guild of Pepperers had been formed, which in 1345 became the Worshipful Company of Grocers. England had also been increasing her sea power and in 1577 Sir Francis Drake, trying to find a north east passage to China, sailed round the world and brought home cargoes of spices from the Moluccas. More and more English traders travelled to the area until, in 1600, the trade was so great that Queen Elizabeth granted a charter to the East India Company to handle our trade with the eastern hemisphere. For the next two centuries there was great rivalry between the Dutch and English for control of the lucrative spice trade and this led to much bitterness between the two countries, not to mention the Portuguese and the natives of the Malay states.

In the late 17th century the Dutch virtually monopolised the clove trade by growing the trees on their island of Aboyna and ensuring their monopoly by destroying trees found elsewhere. However, in 1749 a Frenchman obtained some mother cloves (ripe fruit) fit for planting and he managed to smuggle these away and plant them in the islands of Madagascar and Zanzibar, and consequently, the bulk of the world's cloves today come from these two islands.

With the growth of colonisation most of the spice producing areas came under British, French or Dutch rule and influence, and so followed a period of great prosperity.

Today these countries having gained their independence, rely to a great extent on their spice crops for a healthy economy. Nutmegs, for example, are practically the sole export of the island of Grenada, whilst cloves provide the main export of Zanzibar and Madagascar. The journey time today by modern cargo-ship is a matter of weeks from the Far East to London or Liverpool—a far cry from the year's perilous voyage of our ancestors.

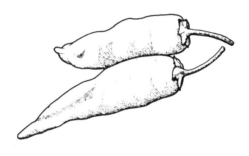

HERBS AND SPICES – WHAT'S THE DIFFERENCE?

This frequently asked question often causes confusion. Usually, spices are the root, bark or berries of plants grown in tropical zones, whilst herbs are the leaves of plants growing in temperate climates. This, however, is not always the case because herbs and spices are culinary terms, not scientific. The line of distinction between the two is therefore somewhat hazy. Mrs Beeton, for example, referred to onions, carrots and turnips as herbs. Even as recently as fifty years ago they could be purchased as such from grocers.

Generally, it is the area where the plant is grown that determines which category it falls into, rather than the part of the plant utilized. Coriander, for example, would be considered a herb if the leaves were used, and a spice if the seeds were required. Therefore, anything that grows within 20° either side of the equator becomes a spice, and plants grown in temperate regions become herbs.

Spice has been defined as 'that which enriches or alters the quality of a thing, especially in a small degree'. The Oxford Dictionary defines a spice as 'an aromatic or pungent vegetable substance used to flavour food'. We at Bart Spices like to refer to our whole range as spices, with culinary herbs being only one group. They are all natural flavouring agents of plant origin.

WHAT IS THE BEST WAY TO STORE SPICES?

The importance of good storage is often underestimated. Direct exposure to light results in loss of colour, and to heat, in loss of aroma. Although most households display their spice collection under bright lights on a kitchen work surface, this is not recommended. Ideally, a cool, dark place such as a larder or cupboard is best. Bunches of dried herbs hung from kitchen ceilings look very pretty, but will be sadly lacking in flavour after a few weeks.

Glass is the best medium for storage. Paper bags tend to absorb the oils responsible for flavour, whilst plastic cause 'sweating' if not scrupulously clean and dry. The lids should be airtight, to prevent the loss of volatile oils and to avoid the ingress of moisture. Snap-on lids are more air-tight than screw-tops, where the screw 'threads' can provide a passage into the jar.

Spices should be purchased in small amounts, or decanted from bulk into smaller jars if these are to be put on display. The contents should be sniffed occasionally to check freshness. Once the aroma has disappeared, it is a false economy to persevere with their use. The flavour will have deteriorated as well, and it is better to throw them away and buy more.

Ground spices are convenient, but for a far superior taste and better keeping qualities, whole spices are unbeatable. They can be freshly ground when required, and remain 'packaged' as nature intended, with their volatile oils intact. Ground pepper is an example. During the grinding process, almost all the volatile oils are lost, leaving only the 'hotness'. Ground pepper adds nothing in the way of flavour to food, where as freshly ground pepper can totally transform a dish. The same can be said of all freshly ground spices.

With herbs, the opposite is true. Their use and concentration increases on drying. In Britain, fresh herbs are often difficult to come by and expensive, although it is now possible to buy them all year round.

Fresh herbs come into their own used as a garnish but give little flavour during the cooking process. Their shelf-life is limited and any attempt to dry them in an oven—often suggested by cookery books—will result in a loss of flavour and aroma. This is because herbs must be dried within an hour or two of cutting to preserve the volatile oils. The herbs you buy fresh from supermarkets are already a day or two old and have started to deteriorate.

Spice growers not only buy their herbs from the best growing regions to ensure excellent quality, they also have the ability to dry their herbs within hours of cropping. Doing this, they are able to drive off the moisture without touching the volatiles, greatly improving the flavour profile. Bearing in mind that a vast amount of the fresh leaf is required to produce a single jar of dried herbs, they are obviously better value than their fresh counterpart, too!

HOW TO COOK WITH HERBS AND SPICES

When spices should be added during cooking, varies from dish to dish. It is best to experiment, but as a general rule, ground spices tend to give up their flavour quickly and should be added towards the end of a long cooking period, whereas whole spices can be added at the beginning and removed just before serving. When grilling or roasting, spices can be rubbed into the surface of the meat or fish, or herbs sprinkled on top.

When preparing a dressing or dip, the spices should be added several hours before serving to allow for full development of flavour. All spices become more aromatic if placed on a baking sheet for ten minutes and heated to 150C (300F, mark 2).

The increased use of freezers is also relevant to the use of spices in cookery. Ice crystals which form during freezing can rupture cell walls and release otherwise trapped flavour constituents. Spiced foods will therefore have an increased flavour on re-heating and this should be remembered when cooking for freezing. Also remember the strength of the spices will continue to develop over time. Up to two months' storage will make little difference, but anything over this period will produce an unfavourable comparison with the original taste. Wherever possible, it is best to add spices after thawing or during re-heating.

The effect of heat is two-fold. On the one hand, tissues and cell walls are broken down, so the flavour is released. On the other, however, volatile oils are driven off so the flavour can be lost. You must be aware of these processes so you do not spice too lightly or too heavily. For the best flavour development, a long, slow cooking period in a sealed casserole dish, is probably best.

Remember these points to get the best from your spices:

- The word spice does not mean 'hot'. Very few can be classified in this manner: most are quite mild and have only a subtle flavour.
- Be careful to use just the right amount, unless you particularly require a dominant taste. Sometimes restraint can produce a better result than being heavy-handed: flavour does not necessarily increase in direct proportion to the amount used.
- Please experiment, for as long as the basic ingredients of a recipe remain unchanged, the addition of spices will not change its nature.
- Become familiar with the flavours associated with all the various spices. In time you will know instinctively which spice to use to achieve a desired taste.

PRESERVATION OF HERBS AND SPICES

Air drying

This is an ancient and established method for preserving a wide range of foods. Historically, in warm Mediterranean countries most herbs and spices were air-dried using the heat of the sun. To some extent this is still the case, but, although most herbs are easily grown in the United Kingdom, the commercial cost of drying them is too great to make it worthwhile.

A modern alternative method to air drying is freeze drying.

Freeze drying

To illustrate the basic principle of this process think of what happens if you dry wet laundry on a frosty day. The water in the clothes turns to ice, making them stiff, then changes from the solid to the vapour state without passing through a liquid state phase and the washing becomes dry without the ice having melted. Although not a cheap process, if freeze drying is successfully carried out, the final product is so little altered that when moisture is added the herb is at once restored to its original state.

Freeze-dried products, if suitably stored in air-tight containers, can be kept for long periods, but, for best results, use the contents as soon as possible after opening and make sure that the jar cap is firmly closed to prevent moisture entering the jar.

Bart Spices' freeze-dried range
- Basil
- Chives
- Dill tops

- *Fines herbes*
- Oregano
- Parsley
- Tarragon

These herbs offer a richer colour and better flavour than conventional air-dried herbs.

THE RANGE OF HERBS AND SPICES

Allspice (Pimenta officinalis)
Allspice is the dried fruit of an evergreen tree native to the West Indies and the neighbouring coast of continental America. In spite of its name, allspice is not a mixture of spices but the berries of the allspice tree. The name comes from the flavour which is reminiscent of combined cloves, cinnamon and nutmeg.

Allspice is used in marinades, meat, fish and curry dishes where a spicy flavour is desired. It is also used in Christmas puddings, and is found in Benedictine and Chartreuse liqueurs.

Arrowroot (Maranta arundinacea)
This delicate, nutritive starch takes its name from the American Indian word for flour-root, *araruta*. It is a combination of starchy extracts obtained from the roots of various tropical plants and is most often used as a thickening agent.

Basil (Ocimum basilicum)
Known also as sweet basil, basil is a native of India and some north Mediterranean countries. It has a delicate flavour and can be used quite generously with almost all tomato dishes, with peas, beans, potatoes and in green salads. It goes well with most meats and sausages and can be used with fish and in stews, casseroles and soups. Many people like to add it to scrambled eggs and cheese. Italians add it to pizza.

Basil's name has two conjectural sources. One suggests it comes from the Greek *Basileus*, meaning king. The Greeks thought only the king should cut basil leaves, using a golden sickle. The other derivation is from 'basilisk', a mythical Greek creature in lizard-like form which was thought to be able to kill its victims by simply looking at them.

The basil plant is an annual of the mint family. Today, it comes principally from Hungary, Indonesia, Morocco, France and America. It is a small bushy plant that grows profusely and up to 2 ft (60 cm) high. The leaves are glossy and greyish-green. The flowers are a purplish white. To harvest basil, the branches are cut off just before the flowers are due to appear, but by cutting back only part of the way to the ground there is often a chance of a second crop.

As well as its culinary use, basil is an important ingredient in the Chartreuse liqueur, and has been used in snuffs.

Bay leaves (Laurus nobilis)

The leaves come from the bay tree, a member of the laurel family, which is native to the Mediterranean and certain parts of Asia. It is grown commercially today in the Far East, the Mediterranean and parts of Turkey, as well as Greece, France, Belgium and America.

In cooking, bay leaves, which can be used whole, cut up or ground, give a strong pungent flavour, and the whole leaves are usually removed before serving. Bay leaves are useful in soups, with steamed or boiled fish, with mince, stews, casseroles and in sauces and gravies. Whole or cut, bay leaves are used in pickling spice, and are often used when boiling vegetables. The bay tree grows up to 4.8 m (18 ft) high. The highly aromatic leaves are a dark green in colour and glossy on top. They can be up to 7.5 cm (3 in) long, stiff and brittle. The leaves are harvested by hand and are dried in trays under slight pressure to prevent curling.

Black pepper (Piper nigrum)

The history of the spice trade is, above all, the history of pepper. Legends lead us to believe pepper was already moving westward from India some 4000 years ago. Ancient Greeks and Romans used both black and white pepper. Our word for pepper is derived from the Latin piper, which in turn comes from the Sanskrit pippali. The Latin not only gave us our English word pepper but *poivre*, *Pfeffer*, *pepe*, *pimenta* and *pepper* in French, German, Italian, Spanish and Swedish respectively.

Pepper is the native of the hot jungle lands never more than 20° from the equator. Both black and white pepper are derived from the same perennial climbing shrub *Piper nigrum*, which many believe to be a native of Malabar, a region on the west coast of India. The bulk of the world's supplies today come from India, Indonesia, Sarawak, Ceylon and, from the first country in the western hemisphere to produce pepper, equatorial Brazil.

Though both berries are borne of the same vine, there is a difference between black and white pepper. Berries to be used for black pepper are picked just before they are fully ripe and then dried in the sun. Those to be used for white pepper are allowed to ripen completely. This makes the removal of the outer skin easier, leaving the inner kernel which, when ground, makes white pepper. Black peppercorns retain the dark outer covering which makes them more pungent than white pepper. In England, more white pepper than black is used, whilst in the United States and on the continent the reverse is the case.

Boston grain pepper
A fine quality, ready-to-use pepper, so-named after a New England-style pepper. It is excellent sprinkled over prepared food and can also be used during cooking. It is absolutely perfect with smoked salmon.

Bristol Blend Five Peppers
A combination of black, green and white pepper with pimento and pink pepper, the latter being a speciality of Reunion Island, Indian Ocean. Five peppers are very colourful and, for the best effect, they should be used at the table in a clear peppermill.

Caraway seeds (Carum carvi)
These are the dried ripe fruit of a biennial plant, the existence of which has been known in northern Europe for thousands of years. For the past century, Holland has been growing caraway on the heavy clay land which it managed to wrest back from the sea and

today supplies the bulk of imports into the United Kingdom. The seeds are used in certain cakes and bread and, when ground, to make Kümmel, a German, Danish and Dutch liqueur.

Cardamom (Elettaria cardomum)
Cardamoms are the dried seeds of a plant in the ginger family. It is cultivated mainly in India, Ceylon and Indo-China and is used for flavouring purposes. The Indians use most of their crop as it is a favourite seasoning for their curries, desserts and after-dinner sweetmeats. The Scandinavian countries are also large users of cardamoms—they were introduced there by Vikings—and Scandinavian cooks add 2.5 ml (½ teaspoon) ground cardamom to a cupful of sugar and sprinkle it on top of their baked goods.

Capsicums
These are the fruits of the various plants belonging to the genus *Capsicum*. From the very beginning, these pods were misnamed 'peppers', although they are in no way related to the true peppercorn. They come in a wide variety of sizes, shapes and colours, and their pungency ranges from sweet and mild to very fierce. Among the latter are ground cayenne, a blend of several types of cayenne pods which are mixed and then ground. Others are chilli powder and paprika, which are used in many Italian, Mexican and Hungarian dishes.

Chives (Allium schoenoprasum)
The chive is a small, grass-like hardy perennial about 15–30 cm (6–12 in) high and is similar, though smaller, to the onion. It has multiple flowers and upright bottom leaves.

Chives flourish in the cooler climate of the northern hemisphere and are grown commercially in Germany, England and Scandinavia. The sliced leaves of the plant are used as a herb, but not the small, white bulbs. The leaves give a delicate, onion-like flavour to salad dressings, potatoes, tomatoes, cheese dishes and seafoods. The flavour goes well with omelettes and other egg dishes, in soups and with fishcakes and pies.

As well as being an air-dried herb, chives can be freeze-dried;

this form has gained considerable popularity in America.

Cinnamon *(Cinnamomum zeylanicum)*

Cinnamon is the bark of a tree, a native of Ceylon, which still supplies about two-thirds of the world's needs, but cultivation is also being encouraged in the Seychelles. The tree is a medium-sized evergreen, and the bark is harvested during the rainy season, which makes it more manageable. During the drying process the thin bark curls up into what are known as quillings.

Cinnamon is mentioned in the Bible several times. For instance, in Proverbs chapter 7, there is an account of the woman seducing a young man by promising him her couch has been scented with 'myrrh and cinnamon'. The ground product is used in baking and as a flavouring generally.

Cloves *(Eugenia caryophyllata)*

Cloves are the dried unopened flower buds of the evergreen clove tree, a native of the Moluccas, but which has long since been established in other tropical countries, particularly Zanzibar and Madagascar. These countries produce almost all the cloves in the world. The buds are picked in clusters from the tree and dried ready for use. As each tree produces only a small number of buds, it is easy to understand the high price of cloves.

In Europe and America, cloves are used both whole and ground, not only as a flavouring for food but also for the distillation of an oil used to manufacture perfumery and medicines.

Coriander *(Coriandrum sativum)*

The seeds are the fruit of the plant. Indigenous to the Mediterranean region and southern Europe, it is also cultivated in the Soviet Union, India and Morocco. The seeds are an important ingredient of curry powder and certain medicines. They are also used as a flavouring in drinks and confectionery.

Coriander is one of the very old spices. It grew in the hanging gardens of Babylon, was amongst the medicinal plants mentioned in the Medical Papyrus of Thebes, written about 1550 BC, and coriander seeds have been found in Egyptian tombs.

Cumin (Cuminum cyminum)

Cumin seeds are the fruit of the plant native to the Mediterranean, upper Egypt and Arabian regions. It is widely cultivated in India for curry powder and used also in many native medicines.

Again, cumin is one of the very old spices. It is mentioned in the Bible—Matthew 23.23, 'For ye pay tithes of mint, anise and cumin'. As well as its use in curry powder, it is used commercially either whole or ground in the preparation of meats, pickles, sausages and soups.

Curry leaves (Murraya koenigii)

These come from the small curry-leaf tree, a relative of the lemon tree, which produces a hard useful wood and fragrant aromatic leaves. It is indigenous to tropical Hindustan at the foot of the Himalayas. These leaves are one of the ingredients used in curry blends and impart a delicate curry flavour of their own.

Curry powder

This is not the ground product of a single spice, but of many spices. The basic ingredients are usually turmeric, coriander, cumin and fenugreek, to which all or some of the following spices are added—cayenne, ginger, cardamom, allspice, cloves, fennel, black and white pepper. The choice of spices depends on the culinary purpose for which the curry is to be used, and whether a hot or mild curry is preferred. Many delightful dishes can be prepared with curried rice, meat, chicken, fish and eggs. A little curry powder added to soups and stews will give them an added note of flavour.

Dill tops (Peucedanum graveolens)

As a herb, this annual is often overlooked, but it imparts a lovely flavour, especially to fish dishes. It has a faintly sweet taste and is particularly good with freshwater fish. It is often used with cucumber to accompany salmon and is commonly associated with dill pickles.

Fennel seed (Foeniculum vulgare)

The fennel plant is native to southern Europe and Asia Minor. Fennel has a stronger flavour than dill, to which it is closely related, although it is more aromatic and sweet smelling.

The dried fennel seeds are usually greenish or yellowish-brown, and resemble tiny watermelons. They emit an agreeable, warm sweet scent, somewhat similar to anise. The seeds are highly acclaimed for their digestive properties and are therefore good with hard-to-digest foods such as oily fish. Fennel is often referred to as 'the fish herb'. Other uses include marinades, soups, sauces and salads.

Fenugreek (Trigonella foenum-graecum)

The small yellow-brown beans are used as a spice. Fenugreek has been used since very early times for cooking and medication, and is still cultivated in some places for its medicinal properties. It is widely grown in areas where there is malnutrition, as it has recognized body-building properties and is cheap and heavy cropping. Fenugreek is found in most curry blends. Use it in chutneys and pickles, where its slightly harsh flavour blends in well.

Galangal (Languas galanga)

The dried, tuberous root of a plant native to south-east Asia. This ginger-like rhizome is dried and sliced. It should be soaked in water before grinding with other curry spices to make a paste. It is excellent in a spicy barbecue marinade, as it gives a hot ginger flavour with a sweet note.

Garlic (Allium sativum)

Garlic is one of the most powerful seasoning agents around, and has been revered for centuries for culinary and medicinal use. Its name is derived from the Anglo-Saxon garleac or 'spearplant'. The composite bulb consists of several small egg-shaped bulbs, termed cloves, enclosed in a white membranous skin.

In many very hot countries people eat garlic daily to prevent such diseases as typhus and cholera. Garlic's essential volatile oil has strong antiseptic and germicidal properties.

Garlic can either be chopped directly into a dish or, for a subtler flavour, rubbed around the outside of the cooking utensil. Garlic may be used in almost any meat, fish or vegetable dish to good effect.

Garlic grain pepper

Use wherever the flavours of garlic and black pepper are required.

Ginger (Zingiber officinale)

Ginger is the washed and sun-dried tuberous root of the herbaceous perennial plant native to tropical Asia, but now grown in Jamaica, India, Africa and China. Ginger was one of the first authentic, oriental spices to be introduced to the western world. This probably occurred about the first century AD, as ginger is in recipes of the period.

Jamaica grows the best-quality ginger. It is used, when ground, in high-class cake and biscuit making. It is also used by mineral water manufacturers, the root being crushed and then distilled for the ginger essence. African ginger is used for the same purpose but generates more heat and is not as delicate in flavour as Jamaican ginger.

Chinese ginger is mainly used to produce crystallized or preserved ginger. The root is partly dried, then boiled in syrup, packed into bottles or jars and sold in this country as a confection, not a spice.

Green pepper berries (Piper nigrum)

These are picked unripe from the pepper vine before the berry has formed its hard core. They are dried quickly to preserve their unique flavour and are valued for steak *au poivre*. They can also be used to good effect in Indian cooking and added to black peppercorns in a peppermill.

Juniper berries (Juniperus communis)

This spice is the fruit of a shrub native to the British Isles. For many years it was considered a magic plant, woven about with superstitions, and also a powerful protection against epidemics.

The small black berries are aromatic with a pine tang. For maximum flavour, they should be crushed before adding to a dish. Juniper is a major flavouring agent in gin, and in cooking is used with venison, game, pâtés, sauerkraut and pork dishes.

Lemon grain pepper
A ready-to-use blend of black pepper and dried lemon. It is recommended for use wherever pepper is added and the flavour of lemon is required.

Lemon grass (Cymbopogon citratus)
This is the bulbous base cut from a grey-green grass native to Indonesia, Malaysia, Sri Lanka and Thailand. As it is dried and sliced, lemon grass is fairly hard and should be soaked in water before use. As the name suggests, it has a distinctive lemon fragrance and is used in the Thailand soup delicacy 'tom yam', extensively in curry dishes and salads and on grills. It is often used in making curry spice paste and is excellent in marinades, sauces and chutneys.

Mace and nutmeg (Myristica fragrans)
Both are products of the same tree, a native of the Moluccas but which now grows freely in both the East and West Indies. The tree is an evergreen, grows to a height of about 8 m (25 ft) and will produce a crop of about 1000 nutmegs a year during its lifespan of 60 years. The fruit is not unlike a peach in appearance, and when ripe it splits in half, leaving the nutmeg in the shell with the mace around the outside of the shell. The mace is removed and dried in the sun. The shell is then cracked and the nutmeg extracted. Both are used exclusively in the manufacture of cooked meats. Ground nutmeg is used in the kitchen to flavour milk puddings and custard.

Marjoram (Origanum majorana)
Also known as sweet marjoram, this is the perennial herb of the mint family (Labiateae). It is grown principally in Mediterranean regions, as well as Portugal and France. Historically, marjoram was prized as a herb to sweeten the air, and was often strewn on the stone floors of great houses and castles.

Mint (Spearmint—Mentha spicata; Applemint—Mentha rotundifolia)
Mint is a plant which grows right across the temperate zones of the world. The main commercial growing countries are now England,

France, Egypt, Argentina, Rumania, Russia, Bulgaria and Morocco.

As a kitchen herb, the dried leaves are used in mint sauces for veal and lamb dishes, with new potatoes, carrots, marrows and with creamed cheese, baked and grilled fish. Its sweet and delicate flavour adds to the taste of these dishes without any risk of the original flavour being lost. Mint leaves are also used for making mint tea and in distillation processes. Mint oils are widely used in confectionery, perfumes, pharmaceuticals and mint liqueurs.

Mustard seed (Black—*Brassica nigra*; white—*Sinapis alba*)

Mustard is one of the oldest condiments known. Mustard seed can be grown in most temperate climates and is widely cultivated today in Argentina, Australia, Canada, China, Denmark, England, Ethiopia, France, Italy, India, the Netherlands, Poland and the western parts of the United States.

Mustard comes from the black or white seeds of the mustard plant. Black seeds give aroma and white ones give pungency. Most mustards are a combination of the two in varying proportions. The seeds are ground to make a mustard flour (except in certain blends like the French *Moutarde de Meaux*) and the special flavours that differentiate the various types are produced by the liquid which is used to moisten the flour. The whole seeds are used in pickling or boiled with vegetables—cabbage and sauerkraut, for example.

Oregano (*Origanum vulgare*)

Confusingly, oregano is also called wild marjoram. Originally grown and used mainly around the Mediterranean, oregano is now used increasingly in England because of the popularity of pizza and other Italian food.

The herb can be used to flavour vegetables, cheese dishes, stuffings, soups and sauces. It is excellent with tomatoes, pasta and salads. The principal growing areas are now Portugal, France and the Mediterranean areas.

Oregano is often one of the herbs in mixed herbs and Italian Seasoning. It has a strong flavour and should be used with discretion.

Parsley (*Petroselinum crispum*)

Parsley is a biennial herb but, since its foliage is the harvested item, it is now grown as an annual. Most of the parsley used in England is English grown. It needs plenty of water to encourage the growth of dense foliage, but to preserve the flavour the leaves of the plant need rapid drying when picked. As a dried product, the demand for parsley has increased considerably and it is now available all year round.

With a mild and agreeable flavour, parsley is a popular kitchen herb. Use it either as a flavouring, or a garnish for salads, meat, fish, poultry, sauces, soups and gravies. It is excellent in cheese and egg dishes, and complements most vegetables. It is good in stuffings, casseroles, dumplings and as a sauce with melted butter.

Parsley is rich in vitamin C, iodine and iron, and it is usually included in mixed herbs and bouquets garnis.

Poppy seed (Papaver somniferum)
The seeds come from the opium poppy, indigenous to the Eastern Mediterranean and Asia.

The tiny poppy seeds, which have an agreeable nutty flavour and no narcotic properties, are used as a condiment on rolls, pastry and baked goods, or crushed to produce an edible oil. They are used widely.

Rosemary (Rosmarinus officinalis)
Rosemary is a small evergreen shrub, native to the Mediterranean, with small and narrow leaves. When dried, they are a fragrant seasoning herb. Although one of the traditional English herbs, the commercial crops of rosemary now come primarily from France, Spain, Portugal and North Africa.

The leaves of the shrub must be dried as soon as possible after harvest. They are pale green with a clean, fresh bittersweet flavour. The chief kitchen uses for rosemary include lamb dishes, soups, stews, marinades, poached and boiled fish, seafood and most boiled vegetables. It is sometimes included in bouquets garnis and in mixed herbs. Take care when using, as too much can overpower the other ingredients in a recipe.

Sea salt
Salt has been used by man since the beginning of time. The impor-

tance of salt in everyday life is reflected by phrases such as 'worth his salt' and 'salt of the earth'. The word salary derives from salt money paid to Roman soldiers over 2000 years ago.

Before refrigeration, bottling and canning, one of the few methods of preserving food such as vegetables, meat and fish was to 'salt it down'. Sea salt, as opposed to rock salt, retains valuable sea-water trace elements such as magnesium and calcium.

Saffron (Crocus sativus)

Saffron is the world's most expensive spice because it takes the stigmas of about 75,000 crocus blossoms to make 450 g (1 lb) of saffron. Its origins probably lie in the Holy Land. From the Song of Solomon we learn it was among the chief spices. The Greeks and the Romans called the little bulb *krokus*, and the Romans introduced it all over Europe. The Moors took it to Spain, and today many Spanish recipes feature saffron. It is a spice to be used very sparingly; just a few strands give excellent colour and aroma to a pot of rice.

Sage (Salvia officinalis)

Sage is a hardy evergreen shrub that originated in the Mediterranean area. The dried herb is prepared from the leaves of the plant and is grey-green. It is a strong, aromatic herb with a bitter afternote.

Commercial crops come principally from Yugoslavia, Italy and England. Its chief cooking use is with fatty meats such as pork and sausages and as a seasoning for poultry. The meat processing industry is a large user. It can also be used in soups and sauces and with cheese, vegetables and tomatoes. Sage is a strong-flavoured herb and should be used with discretion.

Sesame seeds (Sesamum indicum)

Sesame is an annual herb indigenous to Indonesia and tropical Africa. It has, however, been cultivated since earliest times in most hot countries of the Old World for its small seeds, which contain about 50 per cent of an oil used in cooking.

The seeds are widely used in Eastern cookery, especially on bread, cakes and biscuits. They are also good in salads and sprinkled on cottage or cream cheese. They have a sweet, slightly burnt flavour, which can be heightened by toasting them before use.

Sichuan peppercorns

Sichuan peppercorns are known throughout China as flower peppers because they look like flower buds opening. They are reddish-brown with a strong pungent odour, distinguishing them from the hotter black peppercorns. They are actually not from peppers at all, but are the dried berries of a shrub which is a member of the citrus family. Their smell is similar to that of lavender, whilst their taste is sharp and mildly spicy. They can be ground in a conventional peppermill and are very often roasted before they are ground to bring out their full flavour.

Star anise (Illicium verum)

The star anise, whose oil is liquorice-like in flavour and smell, is a small evergreen tree native to south-western China. When ripe, the hard brown fruits of this tree open out in the shape of a star, hence the name.

Anise is used mainly to flavour cakes and biscuits and anise-based drinks, such as pastis, anisette, Greek ouzo and Turkish raki. Traditionally, the Japanese used ground star anise bark as incense. In the Orient, the seeds are chewed after meals to aid digestion and sweeten the breath, whilst in America, dogs and cats are rapidly getting used to the taste of star anise, since it has become a popular flavouring in pet food.

Tarragon (Artemisia dracunculus)

Tarragon is a small herbaceous perennial plant indigenous to southern Russia and western Asia.

The English word 'tarragon' is a corruption of the French estragon, or little dragon, derived from the Arabic tarkhun. Some writers believe the herb was given this name because of its supposed efficacy in curing bites of venomous reptiles, while others claim the designation alludes to the coiled serpent-like roots of the plant.

Tarragon is now grown commercially in both Russia and France, but French tarragon is superior in terms of flavour and appearance. Available whole or ground, it blends well with tomato juice, *fines herbes* and fish sauces, or may be sprinkled on fresh salads, meats and stews. It has a special affinity for chicken and lobster. Its flavour is so pungently distinctive, however, that it is best to use it sparingly.

Tarragon vinegar, a favourite of culinary connoisseurs, is prepared by saturating the fresh and dried herb in wine vinegar. It creates a tasty salad dressing and adds distinctive flavour to sauces such as béarnaise, tartare and hollandaise.

Thyme *(Thymus vulgaris)*
Well known in herb gardens, thyme has grey and pungent leaves. Originally a native of Mediterranean countries, it is now grown commercially in France, southern Europe and the United States.

Thyme has a warm, aromatic and slightly pungent flavour. It contains strong volatile oils used commercially as antiseptics and germicides. It was these qualities that made thyme part of the traditional Maundy Thursday posy carried by the Queen as a protection against infection. Mixed herbs almost always contains thyme and it is usually found in bouquets garnis. It is a strong-flavoured herb that goes well with the robust flavours of cooked meats and vegetables.

Turmeric *(Curcuma longa)*
Turmeric is the root of this plant, a member of the ginger family. It is a colourful, versatile product, combining the properties of a spice and a brilliant yellow dye. This colouring matter has, for many centuries, been used as a vegetable dye in the Far East to give a rich yellow colour to silks, cottons, foods and even people at times.

In many Asian countries, turmeric is still used medicinally. It may be taken internally as a tonic for treating ulcers or externally as an ointment to heal skin sores. Boiled with milk and sugar, it is taken as a remedy for the common cold.

Ground turmeric lends colour and flavour to prepared mustard and is included in many pickle and relish recipes. Its outstanding use, however, is as a highly important ingredient of most curries, primarily because of the vivid yellow colour it imparts together with a distinctive pungent flavour.

Vanilla pod (Vanilla planifolia)

Vanilla is the cured pod of the climbing orchid tree, native to Central America, but which is now cultivated commercially in other tropical regions, especially Madagascar and Oceania.

Vanilla sugar is the finely ground pod mixed with sugar. Vanilla is the main flavouring in most chocolates and tends to reinforce the characteristic chocolate taste. Some European chefs and French housewives prefer to use the actual pod rather than the extract. Recipes in most French cookery books call for it.

Most vanilla flavour is marketed in the form of pure vanilla extract, widely used as a flavouring par excellence for ice-cream, soft drinks, egg nogs, chocolate confectionery, sweets, tobacco, baked goods, puddings, cakes, biscuits, liqueurs and as an ingredient in perfumery.

White pepper

White pepper is mainly used in sauces or dishes where the colour of black pepper should be avoided, for instance in white sauces, chicken and fish.

BART SPICES' SEASONINGS AND BLENDS

Remember—these are all additive-, colouring- and preservative-free, with the exception of a free-flowing ingredient in salt-based seasonings.

Bouquets garnis
Bouquets garnis for meat include thyme, parsley, bay leaves and marjoram. The blend is encapsulated in infusion sachets for convenience, so they can be removed when serving without leaving herb particles behind.

Bouquets garnis for poultry and fish
These contain parsley, thyme, tarragon, bay, sage and basil.

Celery salt
A combination of sea salt and celery. Add to soups, stews and casseroles.

Chinese five spice
The five main spices used for Chinese cuisine are combined in this blend to give red, cooked meats and poultry dishes an authentic Chinese appeal. The five spices are cinnamon, fennel, star anise, cloves and ginger.

Curry blends
Tandoori – This is blended especially for baked dishes such as tandoori murgha (chicken) but also perfect for marinading and barbecues. The ingredients are coriander, turmeric, fenugreek,

chilli, cumin, garlic, paprika, ginger, black pepper, cloves and salt.

Garam masala – Ideal for use with poultry and meat, it is highly spiced yet subtle and delicate. Ingredients are coriander, black pepper, cumin, turmeric, ginger, chillies, cloves, pimento and mustard.

Vindaloo – Traditionally used to make a hot curry, this is recommended for meat. Ingredients are coriander, black pepper, cumin, chilli, mustard, paprika, ginger, cloves, pimento and salt.

Roghan josh – This is the most subtle and aromatic blend, especially for lamb. Ingredients are coriander, turmeric, cumin, fenugreek, ginger, onion, pepper, chillies and pimento.

Mild Madras – Use in all curries when a milder flavour is preferred.

Hot Madras – Use when a hotter curry is preferred.

Fines herbes
A classic French combination of parsley, oregano, shallots, tarragon, basil, thyme, marjoram and chives. Use in traditional French omelettes and also in mayonnaise.

Garlic salt
Sea salt and garlic powder for seasoning all savoury dishes.

Herbes provençales
Thyme, rosemary, marjoram, savory, oregano, basil and tarragon for the taste of French cuisine.

Italian Seasoning
Gives an authentic taste to pizza and pasta dishes. It's a combination of oregano, basil, thyme, rosemary, sesame seeds and garlic.

Jamaican Pepper
A subtle blend of whole black and white peppercorns, together with Jamaican allspice.

Mixed herbs
Thyme, marjoram, sage, parsley and oregano are the constituent herbs of this blend, for use in all savoury dishes.

Mixed spice
The sweet spices, namely coriander, cinnamon, cassia, ginger, caraway, nutmeg and cloves, lift and warm cakes, biscuits and pastries.

Onion salt
Onion and sea salt for use in casseroles, stews and soups.

Party Dips

Herb and garlic
A blend of garlic, parsley, chives, onion, tarragon, paprika, pepper, rosemary, sea salt and thyme. Use with mayonnaise and yogurt to make a dip for crudités, pitta bread or crisps.

French onion
Parsley, chives, leek, onion, garlic, natural vegetable flavour, paprika, pepper and sea salt.

Seafood
Paprika, parsley, chives, garlic, sea salt and pepper make up this blend.

Curry
A blend of curry powder, parsley, chives, garlic, onion and salt.

Pickling Spice
Coriander, mustard and ginger, pepper, chilli, cloves and pimento provide the perfect blend of spices for use when pickling.

Steak Pepper
Cracked black pepper to pep up a plain grill.

Wine Mulling Spices
Add to warmed red wine. Ginger, cloves, nutmeg and orange peel combined in infusion paper sachets transform ordinary wine into the traditional mulled wine.

QUICK COOKING GUIDE

Although most households these days own spice racks, they are often used only as attractive kitchen accessories.

Spice collections usually get used only if called for in a specific recipe. The average cook seldom looks at the rack when cooking on a day-to-day basis. As most people follow recipes rarely, perhaps only for special occasions, this may mean the spices remain untouched for months at a time. This is a pity; not only because they lose their impact over a long period of time, but also because spices improve *every* dish—no matter how ordinary.

Here is a suggested list of spices for use with every type of food. This will enable you to see at a glance which one is best used to improve the quality of your cooking! Using our guide, for example, you will be able to see freshly ground green peppercorns are delicious with steak, and tarragon goes very well with chicken.

You will, no doubt, discover some interesting combinations, either by accident or design. The list below is only a guide, and if you do make an exciting discovery, please let us know. We would like to hear about it! You can find the recipes on page 47 onwards.

Beef
- Black pepper, green pepper berries, Jamaican pepper, steak pepper—freshly ground on grills
- Chilli powder—mince
- Marjoram, bouquets garnis for meat, bay leaves, garlic granules for stews and casseroles
- Coriander (Barbecued Beef Kebabs p. 57)

- Ginger (Stir-fried Beef and Onions p. 69)
- Mixed herbs
- Thyme

Beverages
- Cinnamon—cinnamon sticks for stirring and ground cinnamon dusted over milky drinks
- Mulling spices—mulled wine
- Tarragon—Pimms and cocktails
- Cloves

Bread
- Poppy seed, sesame seeds, caraway seeds—sprinkled on top
- Cinnamon—mixed with sugar and butter and spread on toast
- Cardamom (Banana Bread p. 86)
- Garlic (Garlic Bread p. 94)

Cakes/biscuits
- Cinnamon
- Ginger (Ginger Shortbread Biscuits p. 84)
- Nutmeg (Easter Spice Biscuits p. 84)
- Sesame seeds (Sesame Sables p. 85)

Casseroles/stews
- Bay leaves, black pepper, bouquets garnis, celery salt, onion salt, garlic, Jamaican pepper, sage, herbes provençales, mixed herbs—all casseroles
- Chilli powder
- Paprika
- Italian seasoning (Chicken Cacciatore p. 80)
- Cinnamon

Cheese
- Paprika, cayenne—dusting over surface of cheese dishes
- Chives, sesame seeds—mixed with, or sprinkled on cottage or cream cheese
- Tarragon, mustard seeds—in cheese sauce
- Mace (Béchamel Sauce p. 88)

- Basil

Chinese Dishes
- Chinese five spice (Peking Braised Lamb p. 65)
- Ginger (Stir-fried Beef and Onion p. 69)
- Cinnamon (Crispy Chicken with Sweet and Sour Sauce p. 66)
- Sichuan pepper (Deep-fried Spiced Fish p. 67)
- Star anise—duck, spare ribs
- Sesame seeds
- Chillies

Chutneys/pickles
- Mustard seeds—mustard
- Pickling spice—pickles
- Turmeric (Piccalilli p. 87)
- Curry powder (Tomato Relish p. 88)
- Coriander (Date and Banana Chutney p. 89)

Fish
- *Fines herbes*, herbes provençales—fish marinades
- Parsley—garnish
- Tarragon—plaice
- Rosemary (Lemon Fish Kebabs p. 92)
- Thyme (Cod Portuguese p. 58)
- Paprika (Tuna Steaks with Potatoes p. 59)

French dishes
- Rosemary (Gigot aux Abricots p. 75)
- Herbes provençales (Skewered Fish p. 76)
- Chives (Iced Cucumber and Chive Soup p. 47)
- Garlic (Garlic Mayonnaise p. 89)
- Fines herbes (Omelette aux Fines Herbes p. 76)
- Tarragon (French-style Chicken p. 77)

Fruit
- Allspice—prunes and figs
- Cloves, cinnamon—fruit salad
- Cardamom—fruit pies

- Black pepper, cinnamon—strawberries
- Ginger—all fruit

Indian dishes
- Roghan josh, Vindaloo, Mild Madras, Hot Madras blends—curries
- Cardamom
- Cumin (Cucumber Raita p. 73)
- Coriander (Dal p. 74)
- Turmeric
- Garam masala (Lamb Kebabs p. 72)
- Paprika

Italian dishes
- Bay leaves
- Basil
- Italian seasoning (Cannelloni p. 54)
- Sage
- Thyme
- Oregano
- Rosemary (Gnocchi di Polenta p. 80)
- Saffron

Lamb
- Black pepper, oregano—sprinkled on chops
- Cumin, garlic—marinades
- Rosemary (Gigot aux Abricots p. 75)
- Mint
- Cloves
- Chinese five spice (Peking Braised Lamb p. 65)

Marinades
- Italian seasoning—vegetables
- Tarragon—chicken and fish
- Ginger—kebabs, fruit
- Allspice—barbecues
- Thyme—pork

- Juniper berries—game
- Rosemary—all meats

Poultry
- Thyme, basil—stuffings
- Rosemary, fines herbes—with roast chicken
- Green pepper berries—with roast duck
- Bouquets garnis for poultry and fish—chicken casseroles
- Cumin, coriander—chicken stir-fries
- Tarragon (French-style Chicken p. 77)
- Marjoram
- Rosemary (Chicken Hotpot p. 58)
- Star anise
- Basil

Puddings/pies
- Nutmeg—grated over milk puddings
- Allspice (Creamed Rice with Sherry p. 83)
- Ginger (Ginger Sponge Pudding p. 83)
- Cinnamon
- Cloves (Apple and Fig Pie p. 82)

Rice
- Turmeric, saffron—for colour
- Cardamom, coriander—for flavour
- Cayenne (Hoppin' John p. 60)
- Coriander

Salads
- Sesame seeds—to add a crunchy texture
- Tarragon—tarragon vinegar for a dressing
- Basil, thyme, chives, mint, garlic—added to French dressing
- Paprika—added to natural yogurt to make a dressing
- Caraway seeds (Rainbow Coleslaw p. 51)
- Cumin (Cucumber Raita p. 73)
- Chives (Potato Salad p. 51)
- Cloves

Sauces
- Cayenne—cheese sauce
- Mace—(Béchamel sauce p. 88)
- Tarragon—Béarnaise sauce
- Nutmeg—tomato sauce
- Chilli (Chilli Sauce p. 90)
- Chives (Tartare Sauce p. 90)

Seafood
- Cayenne, black pepper—dusted over prawns, crab or lobster
- Paprika (Shrimp á la Creole p. 60)
- Saffron
- Garlic (Moules Marinière p. 78)

Soups/stocks
- Bay leaves, saffron—infused in stocks
- Nutmeg (Easy Tomato Soup p. 48)
- Cumin (Gazpacho Andalusian p. 48)
- Parsley (Chicken Chowder p. 49)

Stuffings
- Basil, marjoram, thyme—stuffing for poultry or pork
- Sage—beef stuffing
- Mixed herbs
- Mixed spice

Sugar/chocolate
- Vanilla pods—left in sugar, or as a flavour infusion

Vegetables
- Basil, oregano—tomatoes
- Caraway seeds—cabbage
- Chilli powder—baked beans
- Cinnamon—haricot beans, parsnips
- Ginger—carrots
- Mint—potatoes, carrots, peas
- Garlic—mushrooms

- Nutmeg—mushrooms, spinach, parsnips, creamed potatoes
- Cloves, thyme—onions
- Allspice—red cabbage, beetroot
- Rosemary—leeks

Vegetarian dishes
- Turmeric
- Rosemary
- Basil (Stuffed Courgettes p. 61)
- Ginger (Chick Pea Casserole p. 62)
- Oregano (Vegetable Casserole p. 62)
- Cayenne (Cheese and Lentil Loaf p. 63)
- Coriander (Spiced Almond Risotto p. 64)
- Paprika

PART II: RECIPES USING HERBS AND SPICES

STARTERS AND SALADS

ICED CUCUMBER AND CHIVE SOUP

Serves 4

300 ml (½ pint) yogurt
2 teaspoons freeze-dried chives
¼ teaspoon garlic salt
2 tablespoons white-wine vinegar
1 large unpeeled cucumber, grated
freshly ground salt and black pepper
300 ml (½ pint) ice-cold milk

Stir the yogurt, chives, garlic salt and vinegar into the grated cucumber. Season and chill. Just before serving, stir in the milk, then spoon into bowls and serve.

TOMATO SOUP

Serves 4

1 tablespoon dried onion
3 cloves
1 teaspoon freeze-dried parsley
993 g (2 lb 3 oz) can tomatoes
1 bay leaf
freshly ground salt and black pepper
¼ teaspoon freshly grated nutmeg
50 g (2 oz) butter
3 tablespoons plain flour
450 ml (¾ pint) milk
150 ml (¼ pint) vegetable or chicken stock
2–3 tablespoons single cream
extra cream, to garnish

Combine the onion, cloves, tomatoes with their juice, parsley, bay leaf, seasoning and nutmeg in a saucepan. Bring to the boil, then reduce the heat, cover and simmer 1 hour.

In another pan, melt the butter and blend in the flour to make a smooth paste. Cook 2–3 minutes before gradually stirring in the milk. Bring the sauce to the boil, stirring, then reduce the heat and simmer 5 minutes. Remove the bay leaf and cloves and purée in a blender or food processor and pass through a sieve. Combine with the white sauce and mix together well. Stir in the stock and cream, check seasoning and reheat but do not boil. Just before serving, swirl some more cream over the surface.

GAZPACHO ANDALUSIAN

Serves 6

2 slices white bread, coarsely crumbled
900 ml (1½ pints) water
3 tablespoons wine vinegar
750 g (1½ lb) tomatoes, skinned and coarsely chopped
1 cucumber, grated
50–75 g (2½–3 oz) green pepper, seeded and chopped
150 g (5 oz) onion, coarsely chopped
2 cloves
garlic granules
½ teaspoon ground cumin
1 teaspoon salt

Soak the bread in 300 ml (½ pint) of the water until soft, then beat. Sir in remaining ingredients and leave to soak 3–4 hours. Liquidize, then rub through a fine sieve and chill thoroughly before serving.

CHICKEN CHOWDER   *Serves 4–6*

2–3 rashers bacon, chopped
1 onion, chopped
450 ml (¾ pint) chicken stock
350 g (12 oz) root vegetables, diced
300 ml (½ pint) milk
3–4 tablespoons sweetcorn, drained if canned
175 g (6 oz) skinless cooked chicken, diced
freshly ground salt and black pepper
freeze-dried parsley and paprika, to garnish.

Sauté the bacon in its own fat in a large saucepan until the fat begins to run. Add the onion and continue cooking until bacon is crisp. Stir in the stock, then add the root vegetables and cook 10–15 minutes, cover until vegetables are just tender. Add milk, sweetcorn and chicken and cook until heated through: do not boil. Season, then serve garnished with parsley and paprika.

KIPPER PÂTÉ

Serves 4

450 g (1 lb) kipper fillets
1 bay leaf
1 teaspoon dried thyme
75 g (3 oz) butter
juice of ½ lemon
4 tablespoons double cream, lightly whipped
¼ teaspoon ground mace
freshly ground black pepper
lemon wedges and freeze-dried parsley, to garnish

Place the fish in a frying pan with the bay leaf and the thyme. Cover with water, bring to the boil, cover and simmer gently 5 minutes. Remove the skin and bones from the fish and mash the flesh in a bowl.

Cool, then beat in the butter, lemon juice, cream, mace and pepper. Turn the pâté into a 600 ml (1 pint) serving dish, cover and leave to cool. Garnish with lemon wedges and parsley, and serve with toast.

ANCHOÏADE

Serves 4

1 × 50 g (2 oz) can anchovies in olive oil, drained
milk
1 teaspoon garlic granules
freshly ground black pepper
4 slices wholemeal bread, crusts removed
unsalted butter

Soak the anchovies in milk for 30 minutes, then drain and pound to a paste with the garlic in a pestle and mortar. Season with pepper to taste.

Toast the bread on one side, butter the untoasted side, cut into fingers and spread with the anchovy mixture. Place on a baking sheet and cook at 200C (400F, mark 6) 10 minutes.

RAINBOW COLESLAW   *Serves 4*

225 g (8 oz) white cabbage, shredded
225 g (8 oz) red cabbage, shredded
½ green pepper, seeded and finely sliced
1 large carrot, coarsely grated
150 ml (5 fl oz) soured cream
2 tablespoons mayonnaise
1 tablespoon lemon juice
½ teaspoon caraway seeds
½ teaspoon celery salt
freshly ground black pepper

Toss the cabbages, pepper and carrot together. Combine the remaining ingredients and pour over the cabbage mixture. Stir well and chill before serving.

POTATO SALAD   *Serves 4*

100 ml (4 fl oz) mayonnaise
1 tablespoon lemon juice
1 tablespoon olive oil
freshly ground salt and black pepper
2 tablespoons freeze-dried chives
4 tablespoons chopped leeks
450 g (1 lb) cooked potatoes, sliced

Combine mayonnaise, lemon juice, oil, seasoning and half the chives and leeks. Pour over three quarters of the potatoes and mix thoroughly. Arrange the remaining potato on top and sprinkle with the remaining chives and leeks. Cover and chill 30 minutes before serving.

LIGHT MEALS

HARLEQUIN SOUFFLÉ OMELETTE   *Serves 4*

6–8 eggs, separated
225 g (8 oz) cottage cheese
freshly ground salt and black pepper
1 tablespoon freeze-dried chives
50 g (2 oz) butter

Topping:
red pepper or tomato slices
green pepper slices

Beat the egg yolks with the cottage cheese and seasoning until
smooth, then add the chives. Fold in the stiffly beaten egg whites.
Melt the butter in a large frying pan and pour in the egg mixture
and cook 5–6 minutes, then put the pan under a medium grill and
cook a further 3–4 minutes, until set. Slip out of the pan on to a
hot plate and top with slices of red pepper or tomato and green
pepper. Serve immediately.

CHEESE SOUFFLÉ

Serves 4-6

50 g (2 oz) butter
150 g (5 oz) hard cheese, such as Cheddar, grated
25 g (1 oz) plain flour
300 ml (½ pint) milk, scalded
freshly ground salt and black pepper, to taste
¼ teaspoon paprika
5 egg yolks, beaten
6 egg whites
¼ teaspoon cream of tartar

Preheat the oven to 180C (350F, mark 4). Grease a 900 ml (1½ pint) soufflé dish using a little of the butter. Sprinkle about 4 teaspoons of the grated cheese around the inside and press on to the bottom and sides.

Melt the remaining butter in a saucepan. Remove the pan from the heat and stir in the flour to form a smooth paste. Return to the heat and cook 1 minute, stirring. Gradually stir in the milk. Bring to the boil and cook the sauce, stirring constantly, 2-3 minutes, until it is thick and smooth. Remove from the heat again and beat in the seasoning and paprika, then the egg yolks a little at a time. Set aside to cool slightly.

Whisk the egg whites until they are foamy, add salt to taste and the cream of tartar, then continue beating until they form stiff peaks. Stir the remaining cheese into the egg yolks until thoroughly mixed, then fold in the egg whites. Transfer the mixture into a prepared soufflé dish. Carefully mark a deep circle in the centre of the soufflé and cook 40-45 minutes or until it is lightly browned on top and the soufflé is well risen. Serve immediately.

CANNELLONI   *Serves 3–4*

175 g (6 oz) cannelloni shells
1 onion, chopped
250 g (8 oz) mushrooms, chopped
2 tablespoons olive oil
25 g (1 oz) butter
350 g (12 oz) cooked ham or bacon, diced
50 g (2 oz) Cheddar cheese, grated
1 teaspoon Italian seasoning
freshly ground black pepper
pinch garlic salt

Sauce:
25 g (1 oz) butter
25 g (1 oz) plain flour
300 ml (½ pint) milk
50 g (2 oz) Cheddar cheese, grated
½ teaspoon salt
Nutmeg, freshly grated, to taste

Boil the cannelloni as instructed on the packet, then drain. Fry the onion and mushrooms in the oil and butter until cooked, then add the ham and mix well. Add the cheese, Italian seasoning, salt, pepper and garlic salt. Stuff the cannelloni with the ham mixture and arrange them in a buttered shallow ovenproof dish.

To make the sauce, melt the butter in a pan, stir in the flour and cook gently 2 minutes. Remove from the heat and gradually stir in the milk. Bring to the boil, stirring, and cook 2 minutes. Stir in the cheese and add salt and nutmeg to taste.

Pour the sauce over the cannelloni, sprinkle generously with Parmesan cheese and bake at 180C (350F, mark 4) 30 minutes or until golden.

FETTUCINE CON PROSCIUTTO   *Serves 4-6*

450 g (1 lb) fettucine
50 g (2 oz) butter

Sauce:
100 g (4 oz) prosciutto, cut into thin strips
50 g (2 oz) lean cooked ham, cut into thin strips
175 g (6 oz) garlic sausage, cut into thin strips
3 large tomatoes, peeled, seeded and chopped
½ tablespoon freeze-dried basil
freshly ground salt and black pepper, to taste

Cook the fettucine in boiling water 5–7 minutes, until just tender.

To make the sauce, mix together the prosciutto, ham, garlic sausage, tomatoes, basil and seasoning.

Drain the fettucine and transfer to a warmed serving bowl. Add the butter and toss. Stir in ham mixture to coat the pasta. Serve immediately.

LASAGNE AL FORNO   *Serves 4*

2 × 400 g (14 oz) can tomatoes
60 g (2¼ oz) can tomato paste
½ teaspoon dried marjoram
½ teaspoon dried oregano
1 teaspoon sugar
freshly ground salt and black pepper
100 g (4 oz) lasagne
225 g (8 oz) cooked ham, diced
175 g (6 oz) ricotta or cream cheese
50 g (2 oz) Parmesan cheese, grated
225 g (8 oz) mozzarella cheese, sliced

Combine the tomatoes, tomato paste, marjoram, oregano, sugar and seasonings. Simmer gently about 30 minutes, then add the ham.

Cook the lasagne in boiling, salted water 10–15 minutes, then drain well. Cover the base of a deep ovenproof serving dish with a layer of the tomato sauce, add half the lasagne, put in another layer of the sauce, then cover with the cheese, using half of each kind. Repeat these layers with the remaining ingredients, finishing with a layer of cheese.

Cook at 190C (375F, mark 5) about 30 minutes, until golden. Serve immediately from the dish.

MAIN COURSES

Meat

BARBECUED BEEF KEBABS $\qquad$ *Serves 6*

1 kg (2¼ lb) rump steak, cut into 2.5 cm (1 in) cubes
2 tablespoons vegetable oil
2 tablespoons soy sauce
1 tablespoon clear honey
2 garlic cloves, crushed
1 teaspoon ground coriander
1 teaspoon caraway seeds
¼ teaspoon chilli powder

Place the meat in a large bowl. Mix the remaining ingredients together, pour over the meat and marinate 1 hour, stirring occasionally.

Thread meat on to skewers and cook over a hot grill about 10 minutes, turning occasionally and basting with the marinade, until cooked through.

HOT, SWEET PORK CHOPS $\qquad$ *Serves 2*

2 pork chops, rind and fat removed
salt
¼ teaspoon ground ginger
¼ teaspoon curry powder
2 teaspoons grated orange rind
2 teaspoons mustard
1–2 teaspoons clear honey

Sprinkle both sides of the chops with salt. Mix the dry ingredients together, then make into a paste with the orange rind, mustard and honey. Spread half over one side of both chops and grill under medium heat 6–7 minutes. Turn the chops over and repeat with the other side. Serve hot.

Poultry

CHICKEN HOTPOT

Serves 4

450 g (1 lb) potatoes, peeled and sliced
350 g (12 oz) onions, sliced
350 g (12 oz) tomatoes, sliced
4 chicken portions
150 ml (5 fl oz) stock
dried rosemary
freshly ground salt and black pepper
butter

Put a layer of potatoes into an ovenproof casserole, follow with a layer of onions, tomatoes and then the chicken portions. Add the stock and a light sprinkling of rosemary. Repeat layers of tomatoes and onions and finish with potatoes. Season well and put a small knob of butter on the potato slices.

Cover the casserole and cook at 180C (350F, mark 4) 1½–1¾ hours. Uncover the last 20–30 minutes, if wished, to brown the potatoes.

Fish/seafood

COD PORTUGUESE

Serves 4

4 cod cutlets, trimmed and tied in a neat shape
butter
freshly ground salt and black pepper
450 (1 lb) tomatoes, skinned and chopped
75 g (3 oz) onion, finely chopped
1 clove garlic
¼ teaspoon dried basil
1 teaspoon dried parsley
¼ teaspoon dried thyme
tarragon or white wine vinegar
1 teaspoon sugar

Place cutlets in a buttered, shallow, ovenproof dish and sprinkle with salt and pepper, the tomatoes, onion, garlic and herbs. Pour in equal quantities of vinegar and water to come halfway up the cod.

Cover with foil or greaseproof paper and cook at 180C (350F, mark 4) 30–35 minutes, until it is cooked through and flakes easily. Pour the liquid from the dish into a small saucepan. Stir in the sugar and boil rapidly to reduce by half. Garnish the serving dish with the vegetables around the fish and serve the sauce separately.

TUNA STEAKS WITH POTATOES *Serves 4*

2 onions, chopped
1 garlic clove, crushed
100 ml (4 fl oz) olive oil
3 potatoes, sliced into 1 cm (½ in) rounds
2 small red or green peppers, seeded and cut into strips
freshly ground salt and black pepper
½ teaspoon paprika
4 tuna steaks

Fry the onions and garlic in the oil until soft. Add the potatoes and peppers and fry 5 minutes. Stir in the seasoning and paprika. Add the tuna steaks and fry until they are lightly browned on both sides.

Add water to cover and bring to the boil. Reduce the heat, cover and simmer 15 minutes, until the fish is cooked through and flakes easily. Transfer the mixture to a warmed serving dish and serve immediately.

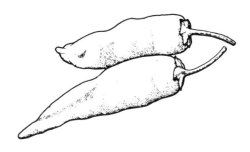

SHRIMP À LA CREOLE
Serves 4

175 g (6 oz) onion, coarsely chopped
1 green pepper, seeded and chopped into 1 cm (½ in) pieces
150–175 g (5–6 oz) celery, finely sliced
50 g (2 oz) bacon fat
400 g (14 oz) can tomatoes
1 teaspoon sugar
3 tablespoons tomato purée
1 clove garlic, chopped
1 teaspoon paprika
¼ teaspoon cayenne
1 bay leaf
350 g (12 oz) shelled shrimps or prawns, thawed if frozen
50 g (2 oz) canned pimento, drained and finely chopped

Fry the onion, green pepper and celery in the fat in a large saucepan until lightly coloured. Add the tomatoes with their liquid and the remaining ingredients, except the pimentos and shrimps.

Cover and simmer gently 25–30 minutes, until the vegetables are tender. Add the shrimps and pimentos and continue cooking 5–7 minutes. Serve with boiled rice.

Vegetarian

HOPPIN' JOHN
Serves 4–6

225 g (8 oz) dried black-eyed beans, soaked in cold water overnight
1.25 litres (2 pints) water
225 g (8 oz) long-grain rice, soaked in water 30 minutes and drained
1 tablespoon vegetable oil
1 onion, finely chopped
400 g (14 oz) can peeled tomatoes
½ teaspoon salt
¼ teaspoon cayenne pepper
½ teaspoon freshly ground black pepper

Put the beans in a large saucepan and pour over the water. Boil 10 minutes, then drain and cover with fresh water. Return to the boil, reduce the heat, half-cover and simmer 1½ hours, until tender. Stir in the rice, re-cover and simmer 15 minutes.

Meanwhile, heat the oil in a frying pan and fry the onion until it is soft. Stir in the tomatoes and their juice and all the seasonings. Pour the mixture into the beans and rice and stir. Re-cover and simmer a further 15–20 minutes or until the rice and beans are cooked and tender.

STUFFED COURGETTES   *Serves 4*

6 courgettes, halved lengthwise
1 garlic clove, crushed
125 g (4 oz) fresh wholemeal breadcrumbs
1 teaspoon dried basil
175 g (6 oz) Cheddar cheese, grated
freshly ground salt and black pepper
2 eggs, lightly beaten
50 g (2 oz) butter, melted

Carefully hollow out the courgette flesh to within 0.5 cm (¼ in) of the skin; keep the shells to one side. Chop the flesh, then press with the back of a wooden spoon to extract as much juice as possible and drain. Set the flesh to one side. Combine the courgette flesh, garlic, breadcrumbs, basil, cheese, seasoning, eggs and half the melted butter until thoroughly blended.

Arrange the courgettes in a well-greased ovenproof dish and stuff with the breadcrumb mixture. Pour over the remaining butter and cook at 200C (400F, mark 6) 20–30 minutes, until the tops are brown and bubbling.

CHICK PEA CASSEROLE

Serves 4-6

225 g (8 oz) dried chick peas, soaked overnight and drained
1 garlic clove, crushed
225 g (8 oz) cabbage, shredded
½ green pepper, seeded and chopped
450 g (1 lb) tomatoes, chopped
1 onion, chopped
1 tablespoon vegetable oil
1 teaspoon ground ginger
pinch ground cloves
1 teaspoon sea salt
freshly ground black pepper
100 ml (4 fl oz) vegetable stock or water

Place chick peas in a large saucepan of water and boil 10 minutes. Drain, cover with more water and simmer 1½-3 hours, until tender.

Meanwhile, fry the garlic and vegetables in the oil until soft. Stir in the ginger, cloves, salt and pepper. Transfer the mixture to a buttered ovenproof dish and stir in the drained chick peas and stock or water. Cook at 180C (350F, mark 4) 20-30 minutes.

VEGETABLE CASSEROLE

Serves 4

2 large onions, coarsely chopped
2 garlic cloves, crushed
vegetable oil for frying
2 green peppers, seeded and chopped
450 g (1 lb) courgettes, thinly sliced
2 aubergines, chopped
225 g (8 oz) mushrooms, quartered
450 g (1 lb) ripe tomatoes, skinned, seeded and chopped
1 × 35 g (2¼ oz) can tomato purée
2 bay leaves
1 tablespoon chopped fresh parsley
½ teaspoon dried oregano
½ teaspoon dried thyme
2 large potatoes, peeled and sliced
25 g (1 oz) margarine

Fry the onions and garlic in the oil in a large flameproof casserole. Add the peppers, courgettes, aubergines and mushrooms and cook 5 minutes, then stir in the tomatoes, tomato purée and herbs. Bring to the boil.

Cover the top layer with the potatoes and dot with margarine. Cook at 180C (350F, mark 4) 1 hour or until potatoes are cooked and brown on top.

CHEESE AND LENTIL LOAF   *Serves 4*

175 g (6 oz) red lentils, picked over and rinsed
350 ml (12 fl oz) water
100 g (4 oz) Cheddar cheese, grated
1 onion, finely chopped
1 tablespoon freeze-dried parsley
½ teaspoon cayenne
a little lemon juice
freshly ground salt and black pepper
1 large egg
3 tablespoons single cream
1 teaspoon butter

Cook the lentils in water, tightly covered, 10–15 minutes, until a stiff purée is achieved. Mix in the cheese, onion, parsley, cayenne, lemon juice, salt and pepper.

In a separate bowl, lightly beat the egg and stir in the cream. Pour this mixture over the lentils.

Grease a 450 g (1 lb) loaf tin with the butter, then press in the mixture. Cook at 190C (375F, mark 5) 45–50 minutes, until the top is golden brown and firm to the touch. If serving hot, allow to stand 10 minutes before cutting.

SPICED ALMOND RISOTTO   *Serves 4*

1 onion, sliced
1 clove garlic, crushed
175 g (6 oz) long-grain brown rice, rinsed and drained
3 tablespoons vegetable oil
3 sticks celery, sliced diagonally
50 g (2 oz) sultanas
100 g (4 oz) mushrooms, sliced
1 red pepper, seeded and cut into strips
100 g (4 oz) blanched almonds
600 ml (1 pint) boiling water
1 teaspoon ground cinnamon
1 teaspoon ground coriander
1 teaspoon ground ginger
freshly ground salt and black pepper
lemon wedges with the edges dipped in paprika, to garnish

Fry the onion, garlic and rice in the oil 5 minutes, stirring frequently. Add the celery to the pan with the sultanas, mushrooms, red pepper, almonds, water and spices.

Bring to the boil, cover and simmer 40 minutes or until the rice is cooked; all the water should by then have been absorbed. Season well and serve hot, garnished with the lemon wedges.

CHINESE CUISINE

Because China has always been a rather poor country with a huge population to support, Chinese cooking tends to concentrate on the practical art of making a little go a long way.

There are five classical regional varieties: Peking and the north, the Yangtze river and the East, Szechuan and the West, Fukien and the southern coast, Canton and the south.

Peking food is rich with dark, strong soy sauce or sweet and sour flavour. To the north of Peking is the only area where lamb is eaten with any enthusiasm.

Light and spicy, Lemon Fish Kebabs (*page* 92) make a special lunch dish.

Ideal for an informal buffet — Mulled Wine (*page 92*),
Anchoïade (*page 50*) and Kipper Pâté (*page 50*).

A very special ploughman's lunch — Cheese and Lentil Loaf (*page 63*) and Tomato Relish (*page 90*).

Creamed Rice with Sherry (*page 83*) is rich, but light, ideally served with crisp biscuits or nuts.

Exotic, attractive and easy to prepare — try Gobi Alu Masala (*page 72*) with Cucumber Raita (*page 73*) for an informal supper dish.

Iced Cucumber and Chive Soup (*page 47*) makes a light refreshing starter on a summer's day. Serve with a swirl of cream.

Hot, Sweet Pork Chops (*page 57*) with Stuffed Courgettes (*page 61*) make an attractive combination of flavours and textures.

Harlequin Soufflé Omelette (*page 52*), served with Rainbow Coleslaw (*page 51*) and Ash Plugged Potato (*page 93*) — a spicy variation on a favourite theme.

PEKING BRAISED LAMB

Serves 4–5

750 g (1½ lb) lean lamb, cut into 2.5 cm (1 in) cubes
1 garlic clove, crushed
¼ teaspoon ground ginger
2 spring onions, chopped
2 tablespoons dry sherry
½ teaspoon Chinese five spice
3 tablespoons dark soy sauce
1 tablespoon sugar

Place the lamb in a saucepan or flameproof casserole. Add garlic, ginger, onions and sherry with just enough water to cover. Bring to the boil, reduce heat, cover and simmer about 1 hour. Add the spice, soy sauce and sugar and cook for a further 30 minutes or until almost all the juice is absorbed.

CRISPY CHICKEN WITH SWEET AND SOUR SAUCE

Serves 4

4 chicken pieces
2 garlic cloves, finely chopped
¾ teaspoon ground cinnamon
freshly ground salt and black pepper
5 tablespoons wine vinegar
vegetable oil for deep frying
3 tablespoons clear honey
1 tablespoon dark soy sauce
2 teaspoons cornflour
2 tablespoons water
chopped spring onions, to garnish

Put the chicken pieces into a saucepan with just enough hot water to cover. Cover the pan, bring to the boil, reduce the heat and simmer 10 minutes. Strain off the water and add the garlic, cinnamon, salt and pepper and the wine vinegar. Cover again and simmer another 5 minutes, then remove the chicken, draining well, and leaving the juices in the pan.

Heat the oil in a deep pan and fry the chicken over a high heat until golden brown all over. Drain well on paper, put into a serving dish and keep warm while making the sauce.

Add the honey and soy sauce to the juices in the pan and stir until the honey is melted. Stir the cornflour into the 2 tablespoons water and add to the pan juices. Bring to the boil and bubble gently 2 or 3 minutes, stirring constantly. Spoon the sauce over the chicken. Just before serving, sprinkle some chopped spring onions on top.

The Eastern part of the Yangtze River has dishes which tend to saltiness, and many ingredients are often in fact, preserved in salt. A lot of fish is eaten here, and rice, not noodles, is the staple accompaniment.

DEEP-FRIED SPICED FISH   *Serves 3–4*

750 g (1½ lb) whole fish, such as sole, cod or halibut, cleaned and scaled
3 spring onions, chopped
½ teaspoon ground ginger
2 tablespoons dry sherry
1 teaspoon salt
vegetable oil for deep-frying
1 teaspoon roasted Sichuan pepper, ground
2 tablespoons sesame seed oil
lemon slices, to garnish

Score the fish with diagonal slashes on each side. Mix the spring onions, ginger, sherry and salt in a dish and add the fish. Marinate 30 minutes, occasionally spooning the sauce over the fish. Heat the oil to 180C/350F and deep-fry the fish until golden brown. Drain on absorbent paper and place on serving dish. Sprinkle with ground Sichuan pepper. Heat the sesame seed oil and pour over fish. Serve hot, garnished with the lemon slices.

LIU YU-PIEN
(Sliced Fish in Wine Sauce) *Serves 6*

575 g (1¼ lb) sole fillets, cut into 5 × 2.5 cm (2 × 1 in) pieces
freshly ground salt and black pepper
½ teaspoon ground ginger
2 teaspoons cornflour
1 egg white, lightly beaten
75 ml (3 fl oz) vegetable oil

Sauce:
2 teaspoons vegetable oil
8 Chinese dried mushrooms, soaked in water for 20 minutes, then
  drained and chopped
75 ml (3 fl oz) dry white wine
50 ml (2 fl oz) chicken stock
1 teaspoon sugar
½ teaspoon salt
2 teaspoons cornflour blended with 3 tablespoons water

Put the fish pieces on a board and rub them with salt, pepper, ginger and cornflour, rubbing well into the flesh. Pour over the egg white and toss carefully to coat the pieces thoroughly.

Heat the oil in a large frying pan. Add the fish pieces, in a single layer if possible, and cook 30 seconds, tilting the pan so the oil flows freely around the fish. Turn the pieces over and cook a further 1 minute. Remove from the heat and pour off the excess oil. Keep fish warm in pan.

To make the sauce, melt the oil in a small saucepan. Add the mushrooms and stir-fry 1 minute. Add the wine, stock, sugar and salt and bring to the boil. Stir in the cornflour mix and cook, stirring constantly, until the sauce thickens and becomes translucent. Remove from the heat and pour the sauce into the frying pan. Stir carefully around the fish and return the pan to moderate heat. Cook, turning the fish pieces occasionally, 2 minutes. Transfer the fish pieces to a warmed serving dish, pour over the sauce and serve at once.

Cantonese is the most popular type of Chinese cuisine in Britain. Many stir-fry dishes originate from here and the light soy sauce, rather than the heavier version, is used. Dim sums and foo yungs are also a large part of Cantonese cuisine.

EGG FOO YUNG

Serves 2–3

4 eggs
1 tablespoon light soy sauce
freshly ground salt
½ teaspoon Sichuan pepper
25 g (1 oz) butter
1 shallot, finely chopped
100 g (4 oz) beansprouts
50 g (2 oz) cooked ham, cut into thin strips

Beat the eggs, soy sauce and salt and pepper together until light and fluffy.

Melt the butter in a frying pan with a flameproof handle. Add the shallot, beansprouts and ham and fry 4–5 minutes, stirring occasionally. Pour in the egg mixture, stir with a fork and leave to set. Preheat the grill to high.

When the bottom of the omelette is set and golden, transfer the pan to the grill and grill until the top is set and lightly browned. Serve at once, cut into wedges.

STIR-FRIED BEEF AND ONIONS

Serves 2–3

1½ tablespoons light soy sauce
1 tablespoon dry sherry
¼ teaspoon ground ginger
1 tablespoon cornflour
225 g (8 oz) beef steak, cut into 2.5 × 4 cm (1 × 1½ in) strips
3 tablespoons vegetable oil
225 g (8 oz) onions, thinly sliced
1 teaspoon salt

Mix soy sauce, sherry, ginger and cornflour together. Add beef and marinate 20 minutes.

Heat the oil in wok or frying pan until hot. Add the onion and stir, then add salt and stir a few more times. Add beef and stir constantly over a high heat. As soon as the beef pieces have separated from each other, arrange on a hot dish and serve at once.

INDIAN CUISINE

In northern India, the waves of various conquerors have left their mark on the cuisine. A dish such as Husaini Kebabs is a direct legacy of the Moghuls, whereas the rice-based dishes, especially pullao are from the Persians. The northern cuisine evolved in the courts of the many royal princelings. It is therefore a cuisine of rich food with spices, herbs and sauces.

In the South, however, outside influences are not so predominant, although the Portuguese have influenced the diet in terms of its hotness and an increased use of rice. The south is mainly Hindu, so vegetarian dishes abound.

TANDOORI MURGHA
(Baked Chicken)   *Serves 2*

1 kg (2¼ lb) chicken, halved lengthwise
4 tablespoons lemon juice
½ teaspoon salt
4 teaspoons Tandoori Blend
25 g (1 oz) butter

Make cuts 0.5 cm (½ in) deep all over the chicken legs and breasts and set aside.

Mix together 3 tablespoons lemon juice, the salt and Tandoori Blend to make a paste. Rub the paste into the cuts and leave 24 hours in a cool place.

Place chicken on a baking tray, breast upwards and add the butter. Cook at 200C (400F, mark 6) 45–55 minutes, basting 2 or 3 times. Remove from oven and sprinkle remaining lemon juice over the chicken. Place under grill a further 5 minutes, until crisp. Serve immediately with fresh green salad and raw onions.

CHICKEN TIKKA
(Spicy Chicken Kebabs)   *Serves 4*

150 ml (5 fl oz) yogurt
4 teaspoons Tandoori Blend

1 small onion, grated
4 chicken breasts, skinned, boned and cut into 2.5 cm (1 in) cubes

Garnish:
1 large onion, thinly sliced into rings
2 large tomatoes, thinly sliced
2 tablespoons chopped fresh coriander leaves

Combine the yogurt, Tandoori Blend and onion. Add the chicken, coat well, cover and marinate in the refrigerator at least 6 hours.

Preheat the grill to high. Thread the chicken cubes onto skewers. Place the skewers on the grill rack and grill 5–8 minutes, turning occasionally, until cooked through. Slide the kebabs on to a warmed serving dish. Garnish with the onion rings, tomatoes and coriander leaves and serve at once.

KOFTAS
(Curried Meatballs)   *Serves 4*

25 g (1 oz) butter
4 teaspoons Garam Masala Blend
450 g (1 lb) lean minced beef or lamb
3 tablespoons natural yogurt
½ teaspoon salt
extra butter for frying
3 tablespoons water

Melt the butter in frying pan, add the garam masala and cook gently 5 minutes. Mix the meat, yogurt and salt together and add to the garam masala and butter. Mix in until doughy and pliable.

Divide into 14–16 pieces and shape into balls. Fry gently in the extra butter until soft, shaking pan but taking care not to break the koftas. Turn them over occasionally. Add the water and cook, covered, until the water has dried up and only butter remains. Serve on a bed of cooked basmati rice.

HUSAINI KEBABS
(Lamb Grilled on Skewers)
Serves 4

1 kg (2¼ lb) boneless leg of lamb, trimmed and cut into 5 cm (2 in)
  cubes
50 g (2 oz) onions, finely chopped
1 teaspoon finely chopped garlic
1½ teaspoon salt
3 tablespoons plain yogurt
8 teaspoons Garam Masala Blend

Place all the ingredients in a bowl and stir together until well
mixed. Cover with foil and marinate 4–6 hours in a refrigerator.

Thread 3 or 4 pieces of lamb on to each skewer and cook 10–20
minutes under a very hot grill, or over well-lit charcoal, until
cooked to taste.

GOBI ALU MASALA
(Curried Cauliflower and Potato in Rich Curry Sauce)
Serves 4

75 g (3 oz) butter
½ teaspoon salt
2 teaspoons Garam Masala Blend
1 small tin tomatoes
225 g (8 oz) potatoes, peeled and quartered
100 ml (4 fl oz) water
1 small cauliflower, broken into florets

Melt butter in a heavy-based frying pan. Add the salt, Garam
Masala Blend and tomatoes and cook 10 minutes. Add the potatoes
and water and simmer 5 minutes before adding the cauliflower.

Cover tightly and simmer about 20 minutes; the vegetables
should be cooked but still remain firm. Transfer the cauliflower
and potatoes to a serving dish and pour the sauce over.

Serve the main dishes with any or all of the following accompani-
ments.

CHAPATIS
(Unleavened Wholemeal Bread)

Makes 12

225 g (8 oz) chapati flour
½ teaspoon salt
175 ml (6 fl oz) cold water
extra chapati flour for rolling

Sieve flour and salt into mixing bowl. Make a well in the centre and pour in almost all the water and mix into a soft dough. Knead for about 10 minutes, gradually adding the remaining water. Cover the dough with a wet towel and leave 20–30 minutes. Knead again 5 minutes, adding flour to your fingers if they become too sticky.

Divide into 12 pieces and shape into balls. Roll out each chapati thinly to about 10 cm (4 in) diameter. Very lightly grease a frying pan and heat. Place chapati on pan over medium heat. Turn chapati over as soon as bubbles appear and cook the other side. Remove pan from heat and 'puff up' chapati over a gas flame, turning quickly so it doesn't burn. Serve immediately.

CUCUMBER RAITA

Serves 4

1 teaspoon coriander seeds
1 teaspoon cumin seeds
300 ml (½ pint) plain yogurt
1 cucumber, peeled and diced
1 teaspoon salt
½ teaspoon freshly ground black pepper

Roast the coriander and cumin seeds in a heavy-based frying pan over a medium heat, stirring 2–3 minutes, until the seeds turn a darker brown. When cool, grind them using a mortar and pestle.

Place the yogurt in a serving bowl and beat well with a fork until smooth. Add the cucumber, salt, black pepper and roasted spices, and mix, reserving a pinch for garnish. Sprinkle with the pinch of spices. Cover and refrigerate 1 hour before serving.

DAL

Serves 3–4

225 g (8 oz) red lentils, picked over and rinsed
¼–½ teaspoon turmeric
2 teaspoons ground coriander
450 ml (15 fl oz) water
¼–½ teaspoon chilli powder
225 g (8 oz) can tomatoes, chopped
salt
50 g (2 oz) butter
1 small onion, sliced

Place the lentils, turmeric, coriander and water in a heavy-based saucepan and bring to the boil, then simmer 20 minutes, until tender. Mash the lentil mixture with a potato masher. Stir in the chilli powder, tomatoes and salt.

Cover and simmer gently about 30 minutes. Remove from the heat and set aside. Melt the butter in a pan and fry the onion until light brown. Serve the dal with the onion mixture poured over.

Rice

Always use good-quality rice. We suggest basmati rice. It is a natural, unrefined product and, therefore, it is necessary to remove any extraneous particles, such as rice husks. Wash the rice thoroughly and drain. Boil for 1 minute in a heavy-based saucepan, using as little water as possible, about 500 ml (15 fl oz) for every 250 g (7 oz) rice. Reduce the heat to a minimum, cover and simmer very slowly until all the water has evaporated. Test by biting through a grain; it should be light and fluffy but still firm.

FRENCH CUISINE

The French put more into the study of food than any other nationality. In France, it has become elevated into an art form. The care taken to find exactly the right cut of meat, the perfect stage of ripeness and the best presentation, is second to none.

There are two strands to French cooking. The first is *haute cuisine*, the second *bourgeois* or provincial.

GIGOT AUX ABRICOTS
(Apricot Stuffed Lamb with Rosemary)

Serves 4

2 kg (4½ lb) leg of lamb, boned

Marinade:
6 tablespoons oil
1 teaspoon dried rosemary
4 tablespoons lemon juice

Stuffing:
large knob lard
4 rashers streaky bacon, chopped
1 onion, chopped
175 g (6 oz) cooked rice
1 stick celery, chopped
50 g (2 oz) no-need-to-soak dried apricots, chopped
2 tablespoons sultanas
1 teaspoon dried rosemary
celery salt
freshly ground black pepper
1 egg, size 3, beaten

Put the meat into a shallow ovenproof dish, just large enough to take the joint. Mix the marinade ingredients together, pour over the meat, cover and leave 2–3 hours or overnight, turning occasionally.

For the stuffing, melt the lard and fry the bacon in a small pan. Add the onion and cook until soft. Add to the rice with the celery, apricots, sultanas, rosemary, seasoning and egg.

Remove the meat from the marinade. Stuff the cavity with the rice stuffing and sew it up with a trussing needle and fine string. Return the meat to the dish and cook at 180C (350F, mark 4) 2½ hours, basting from time to time with the surplus marinade. Place the meat on a hot serving dish, remove the excess fat from the pan juices and serve the juices separately. Serve with green vegetables.

BROCHETTES DE POISSON PROVENÇALES
(Skewered Fish)

Serves 4

750 g (1½ lb) halibut or swordfish steaks, boned
1 tablespoon lemon juice
3 tablespoons olive oil
1 teaspoon herbes provencales
2 lemons, quartered, to serve

Put the fish in a bowl. Pour over the lemon juice and olive oil and stir in the herbes provençales. Leave for 3–4 hours, then thread cubes on to 4 skewers. Grill slowly, turning frequently, basting with the marinade. Serve with lemon quarters.

OMELETTE AUX FINES HERBES
(Herb Omelette)

Serves 1

3 eggs
fines herbes
freshly ground salt and black pepper
butter

Mix the eggs thoroughly, but do not beat. Add the herbs and seasoning.

Melt just enough butter to grease the base of the frying pan. Ensure the butter is at the right temperature; the moment it ceases to fizz and turns brown, it is ready. Pour the egg mixture into the pan, lifting the sides to allow unset eggs to run underneath. Keep the left hand at work with a gentle see-saw motion. Give a final shake and turn out, before completely set.

POULET A L'ESTRAGON
(French-style Chicken)

Serves 3-4

2 tablespoons fresh white breadcrumbs
2 tablespoons chopped fresh tarragon
2 teaspoons salt
freshly ground black pepper
50 g (2 oz) unsalted butter, softened
1 egg, size 3, beaten
2 rashers bacon
1–1.5 kg (2¼–3 lb) oven-ready chicken
150 ml (5 fl oz) chicken stock
150 ml (5 fl oz) dry white wine
25 g (1 oz) plain flour
watercress, to garnish

Make the stuffing by working the breadcrumbs, tarragon and seasonings into the softened butter, adding the egg last. Put a little of this mixture under the skin of the chicken and round the breast and legs. Put the rest inside the bird. Cover the breast with rashers of bacon, place it in a roasting tin, add the stock and wine and roast at 190C (375F, mark 5) 1 hour, basting every 15 minutes. Remove the bacon during the last 15 minutes to let the breast brown.

Place the chicken on a serving dish and keep warm. In a sauce-pan, blend the flour to a smooth paste with a little water and slowly add the chicken juices. Bring the sauce to the boil and simmer 2–3 minutes, stirring. Adjust the seasoning and serve separately. Garnish the chicken with watercress and serve.

MOULES MARINIERE
(Mussels in White Wine)

Serves 4

4 dozen mussels, cleaned
4 shallots, finely chopped
1 teaspoon garlic salt
25 g (1 oz) butter
300 ml (½ pint) dry white wine
1 bouquet garni sachet
freshly ground black pepper
2 tablespoons freeze-dried parsley
4 sprigs fresh parsley

Discard any open mussels. Fry the shallots and garlic salt gently in the butter in a large pan 5 minutes or until golden. Stir in the wine, bouquet garni, pepper and mussels. Cover and cook until the shells open, about 10 minutes and discard any which fail to open. Remove the top shells and place on individual plates. Adjust seasoning in sauce if necessary, and pour over the mussels.

The cooking juice can be thickened with a *beurre manie* if preferred; this is accomplished by blending together 1 tablespoon plain flour and 2 tablespoons butter, and stirring into the juices in the pan after removing the mussels. Bring slowly to the boil and simmer until the sauce thickens. Sprinkle the mussels with parsley and garnish with parsley sprigs.

ITALIAN CUISINE

Italian food is superb, varied and inexpensive. It has strong regional influences as Italy did not become a single nation until the 19th century. Sicily is usually given credit for inventing pasta—the staple of Italian cuisine—although the art of drying and preserving it hails from Naples.

In the north-west, the proximity of France and Switzerland has resulted in an overflow of their cultures into Italy—with dishes such as fonduta (a local fondue) as an example. Lombardy is the rice bowl of the country and here risottos are more popular than pasta.

Venice and Genoa, as sea ports, were among the first to sample the produce and spices of the Orient and are particularly proud of their contribution to Italian cuisine.

PEPERONI RIPIENI
(Stuffed Peppers)

Serves 6

freshly ground salt and black pepper
225 g (8 oz) aubergine, diced
3 large green peppers
3 large red peppers
2 tablespoons olive oil
50 g (2 oz) butter
125 g (4 oz) onions, sliced
1 large clove garlic, crushed
350 g (12 oz) courgettes, sliced
225 g (8 oz) tomatoes, quartered
2 or 3 bay leaves
5 tablespoons dry white wine
freeze-dried parsley, to garnish

Sprinkle 2 teaspoons salt over the aubergine and leave about 30 minutes. Rinse and pat dry. From the stem end of the peppers cut a lid about 2 cm (¾ in) down. Remove the core and seeds. Place the pepper shells and lids in boiling water, bring back to the boil and blanch 2 minutes. Drain the peppers.

When cool, arrange in a lightly oiled ovenproof dish. Heat the oil and butter, add the onion and sauté 2–3 minutes. Stir in the garlic, courgettes, tomatoes, aubergines, bay leaves and 3 table-spoons wine. Season well. Cook until the vegetables have softened but not collapsed, and the liquid is absorbed. Stir frequently to prevent the vegetables from sticking.

Remove the bay leaves, divide the filling between the peppers and replace the lids. Spoon the remaining wine into the base of the dish and cook, uncovered, at 190C (375F, mark 5) 30 minutes.

Remove the lids, spoon the remaining juices over the filling, add a little parsley and replace the lids. Serve hot or cold.

CHICKEN CACCIATORE

Serves 4

2 kg (4½ lb) chicken, cut into joints
plain flour
1 tablespoon olive oil
50 g (2 oz) butter
1 large onion, chopped
1 teaspoon garlic granules
8 tomatoes, skinned and chopped
3 tablespoons tomato purée
1 teaspoon sugar
150 ml (5 fl oz) chicken stock
freshly ground salt and black pepper
225 g (8 oz) button mushrooms, sliced
4 tablespoons Marsala

Coat the chicken with flour and fry the chicken joints in the olive oil and butter until crisp and golden. Remove from the pan and keep hot.

Add the onion and garlic and fry until golden. Stir in the tomatoes, tomato purée, sugar and stock and season well with salt and pepper. Bring to the boil and then replace the chicken. Simmer slowly over a gentle heat 30–45 minutes. Add the mushrooms and Marsala and continue to cook for 10–15 minutes. Serve with hot pasta.

GNOCCHI DI POLENTA

Serves 4

900 ml (1½ pints) milk
175 g (6 oz) cornmeal
1 egg, beaten
100 g (4 oz) Parmesan cheese, grated

Sauce:
50 g (2 oz) butter
50 g (2 oz) cooked ham, finely chopped (optional)
400 g (14 oz) button mushrooms, sliced
100 ml (4 fl oz) dry red wine
400 g (14 oz) canned tomatoes
freshly ground salt and black pepper
1 teaspoon dried rosemary

Bring the milk to the boil, then sprinkle over the cornmeal. Cook about 30 minutes, stirring constantly to prevent it from sticking, until thick. Stir in the egg and cheese. Rinse a baking sheet with water, then pour the mixture on to the sheet and smooth the top. The mixture should be about 1 cm (½ in) thick. Chill 30 minutes.

Meanwhile, melt half the butter in a saucepan. Add ham and cook 3 minutes. Stir in the remaining ingredients and bring to the boil. Reduce the heat to low, cover and simmer 20 minutes.

Remove the mixture from the refrigerator and cut into squares or rounds. Arrange them in a well-greased ovenproof dish. Cut the remaining butter into small pieces and scatter over the top. Cook at 220C (425F, mark 7) 10–15 minutes, until the top is well browned. Serve with the sauce.

PUDDINGS/DESSERTS

APPLE AND FIG PIE

Serves 4

225 g (8 oz) plain flour
pinch of salt
150 g (5 oz) butter or margarine, chilled and diced
750 g (1½ lb) cooking apples, peeled and cored
100 g (4 oz) dried figs, chopped
1 tablespoon plain flour
3 tablespoons sugar
¼ teaspoon grated nutmeg
½ teaspoon ground cinnamon
pinch ground cloves or 3–4 whole cloves
2–3 tablespoons water
milk and caster sugar for glazing

Sift the flour and salt into a bowl, rub in the fat until the mixture resembles fine breadcrumbs. Stir in just sufficient cold water to make a firm dough. Cover and leave it in a cool place 30 minutes.

Meanwhile, slice the apples into a basin, add the figs and sift over the flour, sugar and spices. Mix well together.

Put the apples into a buttered 1.2 litre (2 pint) pie dish and sprinkle 2–3 tablespoons water over the filling. Roll out the pastry and use it to cover the pie in the usual way. Decorate the top with pastry trimmings. Brush with the milk and sprinkle with caster sugar.

Bake at 220C (425F, mark 7) 15 minutes, then reduce the heat to 180C (350F, mark 4) a further 30 minutes. Serve warm.

CREAMED RICE WITH SHERRY   *Serves 4–5*

600 ml (1 pint) milk
75 g (3 oz) short-grain pudding rice
45 g (1½ oz) sugar
¼ teaspoon ground allspice
2 tablespoons sweet sherry
300 ml (½ pint) double cream
50 g (2 oz) flaked almonds, toasted

Bring the milk, rice and sugar to the boil in a saucepan. Simmer gently 20 minutes or until the rice is cooked, stirring occasionally. Remove from the heat and stir in the allspice and sherry. Leave to cool.

Whip the cream until thick but not stiff and fold in the rice. Turn into individual dishes, top with almonds and chill.

GINGER SPONGE PUDDING   *Serves 4*

75 g (3 oz) butter
50 g (2 oz) sugar
1 egg, beaten
150 g (5 oz) self-raising flour
2 teaspoons ground ginger
¼ teaspoon salt
1½ tablespoons golden syrup, plus extra for serving

Cream the butter and sugar together until pale and fluffy. Beat in the egg, golden syrup and sifted flour, ginger and salt.

Turn into a greased and floured 1.2 litre (2 pint) pudding basin. Cover with foil and steam 1½–1¾ hours. Serve with more golden syrup thinned with a little water and warmed.

BISCUITS AND BREAD

GINGER SHORTBREAD BISCUITS *Makes 30–33*

350 g (12 oz) plain flour
30 g (1¼ oz) ground ginger
175 g (6 oz) caster sugar
250 g (9 oz) butter

Sift together the flour and ginger, stir in the sugar and rub in the butter until the mixture resembles breadcrumbs. Knead until smooth.

Turn out on to a lightly floured board and roll out to a thickness of 0.5 cm (¼ in) or less. Cut into circles with a 5.5 cm (2¼ in) cutter. Place on baking trays and bake at 180C (350F, mark 4) 15 minutes or until golden. Cool on a wire rack.

EASTER SPICE BISCUITS   *Makes 15–20*

75 g (3 oz) butter or margarine
50 g (2 oz) caster sugar
1 egg, separated
175 g (6 oz) self-raising flour
pinch salt
¼ teaspoon grated nutmeg
¼ teaspoon ground cinnamon
25 g (1 oz) currants
25 g (1 oz) chopped mixed peel
1–2 tablespoons milk
a little caster sugar

Cream the butter and sugar together until pale and fluffy, then beat in the egg yolk. Sift over the flour with the salt and spices and fold in with the currants and mixed peel. Add a little milk to give a soft dough. Roll out the dough thinly and cut into 6 cm (2½ in) rounds with a pastry cutter.

Put biscuits on a lightly greased baking sheet and bake at 200C (400F, mark 6) 15 minutes. After 10 minutes, brush the biscuits with lightly beaten egg white, sprinkle with caster sugar and continue baking 7–10 minutes at 200C (400F, mark 6). Cool on wire rack.

SESAME SABLES
Makes 24–30

75 g (3 oz) butter, chilled and diced
75 g (3 oz) plain wholemeal flour
75 g (3 oz) cheese, grated
1 tablespoon sesame seeds
freshly ground salt and black pepper
1 egg, lightly beaten
extra sesame seeds for topping

Rub the butter into the flour, then add the cheese and sesame seeds and season well. Form into a dough, wrap in greaseproof paper and chill 30 minutes.

Roll out the dough on a lightly floured board until it forms an oblong about 0.5 cm (¼ in) thick. Cut the dough into 5 cm (2 in) wide strips, brush with the egg and sprinkle with sesame seeds. Cut into triangles, place on a greased baking sheet and bake at 180C (350F, mark 4) 5–8 minutes until they are golden brown.

BANANA BREAD

100 g (4 oz) butter, softened
175 g (6 oz) caster sugar
2 eggs, lightly beaten
¼ teaspoon vanilla essence
275 g (10 oz) self-raising flour
½ teaspoon bicarbonate of soda
¼ teaspoon salt
¼ teaspoon ground cardamom
¼ teaspoon ground mace
3 bananas
75 g (3 oz) walnuts, chopped

Cream the butter and sugar until pale and fluffy and beat in the eggs and vanilla essence gradually. Sift together the flour, bicarbonate of soda, salt and spices and add to the creamed mixture together with the bananas and walnuts.

Turn into a lightly greased 900 g (2 lb) loaf tin and bake at 180C (350F, mark 4) 55–60 minutes. Leave in the tin until cool, then turn out. Serve cut into slices and buttered.

SAUCES, DRESSINGS AND STUFFINGS

PICCALILLI

1.5 kg (3 lb) marrow, diced
450 g (1 lb) cauliflower florets
100 g (4 oz) green beans, sliced
225 g (8 oz) onions, sliced
½ large cucumber, peeled and sliced
350 g (12 oz) salt
150 g (5 oz) sugar
1.2 litres (2 pints) white distilled vinegar
40 g (1½ oz) dry mustard
3 tablespoons ground ginger
3 tablespoons plain flour
2 tablespoons turmeric

Layer all the vegetables with the salt in a large bowl, cover and leave 24 hours.

Drain the vegetables and mix thoroughly. Put the sugar, 900 ml (1½ pints) of the vinegar and the vegetables in a large pan and bring to the boil. Simmer 20 minutes.

Blend remaining ingredients together with the remaining 300 ml (½ pint) vinegar. Stir this into the vegetables and bring to the boil. Cook 3 minutes. Pot and cover with vinegar-proof lids.

BÉCHAMEL SAUCE

50 g (2 oz) onion, quartered
50 g (2 oz) carrots, chopped
25 g (1 oz) celery, chopped
½ bay leaf
2 cloves
4 peppercorns, slightly crushed
¼ teaspoon ground mace
1 teaspoon salt
600 ml (1 pint) milk
40 g (1½ oz) butter
40 g (1½ oz) plain flour

Mix all the ingredients, except the butter and flour, with the milk and bring to the boil. Allow to infuse 30 minutes.

Melt the butter, blend in the flour, and cook 1 minute. Strain the milk, add to the pan and bring to the boil, stirring constantly with a wire whisk. Adjust the seasoning and bring to the boil once more, then serve.

TOMATO RELISH

1.5 kg (3 lb) ripe tomatoes, skinned and chopped
225 g (8 oz) onions, finely chopped
3 sticks celery, finely chopped
cooking salt
½ tablespoon curry powder
1 tablespoon plain flour
½ teaspoon dry mustard
600 ml (1 pint) white wine vinegar
350 g (12 oz) sugar

Sprinkle the vegetables with salt in a large bowl, cover and leave 24 hours. Mix the curry powder, flour and mustard in another bowl and add enough vinegar to make a paste. Drain the vegetables, rinse off excess salt and place them in a preserving pan. Simmer gently until just boiling, then cook a further 5 minutes. Dissolve the sugar in the remaining vinegar and add to the pan. Simmer about 30 minutes, then add the flour paste and cook 2–3 minutes, stirring constantly. Pour into hot, sterilized jars and seal with vinegar-proof lids.

DATE AND BANANA CHUTNEY

6 bananas, peeled and sliced
4 onions, chopped
225 g (8 oz) dates, stoned and chopped
300 ml (½ pint) vinegar
½ teaspoon ground coriander
¼ teaspoon turmeric
¼ teaspoon ground cumin
¼ teaspoon ground ginger
100 g (4 oz) crystallised ginger, chopped
½ teaspoon salt
250 ml (9 fl oz) black treacle or molasses

Put the bananas, onions, dates and vinegar into a saucepan and cook 15 minutes, stirring occasionally, until the onions are soft. Remove from the heat and mash to a pulp. Or, blend to a purée. Stir in the coriander, turmeric, cumin, ground ginger, crystallised ginger, salt and treacle or molasses and return to moderate heat. Cook, stirring occasionally, 15–20 minutes, until it turns brown. Remove from the heat and seal into clean preserving jars.

GARLIC MAYONNAISE

1 whole egg or 2 egg yolks
1 tablespoon wine vinegar or lemon juice
½ teaspoon sugar
½ teaspoon dry mustard
½ teaspoon garlic granules
freshly ground salt and black pepper
150 ml (5 fl oz) olive oil

Ensure all the ingredients are at room temperature. Place all the ingredients, except the olive oil, in a blender and mix thoroughly. With the machine running, pour the oil slowly through the top of the blender. The resulting mayonnaise is not as thick as that made by traditional methods, but the risk of curdling is minimized.

TARTARE SAUCE

150 g (5 oz) mayonnaise
few drops lemon juice
¼ teaspoon freeze-dried tarragon
¼ teaspoon freeze-dried chervil
1½ teaspoon chopped gherkins
1½ teaspoon chopped capers
1 teaspoon freeze-dried chives

Mix all the ingredients into the mayonnaise.

RED CHILLI SAUCE

5 whole chillies, dried and crumbled
3 tablespoons boiling water
400 g (14 oz) can tomatoes, drained with juice reserved
1 onion, chopped
2 garlic cloves, chopped
50 ml (2 fl oz) vegetable oil
2 tablespoons tomato purée
1 teaspoon ground cumin
1½ tablespoons wine vinegar
½ teaspoon salt

Blend the chillies, water and tomatoes in a blender or food processor to a smooth purée. Set aside. Fry the onion and garlic in the oil until soft. Stir in the tomato mixture, the reserved tomato juice and the remaining ingredients and bring to the boil. Reduce the heat to low, cover and simmer the sauce 10 minutes.

SAUSAGE AND PRUNE STUFFING

50 g (2 oz) prunes, soaked overnight in boiling water
75 g (3 oz) onion, finely chopped
40 g (1½ oz) butter
225 g (8 oz) sausagemeat
50 g (2 oz) plain biscuit crumbs
½ teaspoon dried mixed herbs
¼ teaspoon dried oregano
1 tablespoon dry sherry
freshly ground salt and black pepper

Drain the prunes, then remove the stones and cut into small pieces.

Fry the onion in the butter until golden. Add the sausagemeat, biscuit crumbs and herbs and continue frying 4–5 minutes. Add the prunes and sherry and season with salt and pepper.

A BARBECUE PARTY

MULLED WINE

2 sachets mulling spices
1 litre (900 ml) dry red wine
500 ml (15 fl oz) boiling water
sugar to taste
orange slices (optional)

Gently heat the wine, taking care not to boil. Add the spices, water and sugar and simmer at least 10 minutes. Slices of orange may be added before serving.

LEMON FISH KEBABS
Serves 4

750–900 g (1½–2 lb) fillet of halibut or other firm white fish, cut into
   2.5 cm (1 in) cubes
½ teaspoon grated lemon rind
2 tablespoons lemon juice
2 tablespoons vegetable oil
pinch garlic salt
freshly ground salt and black pepper
1 teaspoon dried rosemary
8 bay leaves
pinch ground ginger

Place the fish in a shallow dish. Mix together the remaining ingredients and pour over the fish. Leave for at least 30 minutes.

Thread the fish and pieces of bay leaf on to skewers, strain the marinade and pour over the kebabs. Grill slowly for 10 minutes, turning or basting occasionally, until the fish is cooked through and flakes easily.

ASH-BAKED PLUGGED POTATOES   *Serves 4*

4 baking potatoes
225 g (8 oz) full-fat soft cheese
freshly ground salt and black pepper
vegetable oil
butter for serving

Cut 4 large squares of foil that will enclose the potatoes completely. With an apple corer, cut a plug from the centre of each
potato. Cut off 1 cm (½ in) of each plug at the skin end and
reserve.

   Fill the holes with soft cheese, season and replace the 1 cm (½
in) plug ends. Grease the foil squares well, and wrap each potato
completely in foil. Barbecue for about 45 minutes directly on the
coals, or 65 minutes on the grill, turning occasionally. When
cooked, open the packages and serve with butter.

PARTY DIPS   *Serves 4*

30 ml (2 tablespoons) Bart Spices' Party Dips (Herb and Garlic, French
   Onion, Curry or Seafood)
100 g (4 oz) mayonnaise
100 g (4 oz) natural yogurt

Blend all ingredients together and chill at least 1 hour. Serve with
pitta bread, crudités or crisps.

Other dishes suitable for a barbecue party include Barbecue Beef
Kebabs (page 57); Chicken Tikka (page 70); Husaini Kebabs
(page 72); and Brochettes de Poisson Provençales (page 76).

MUSHROOM BURGERS
Serves 4

25 g (1 oz) butter
2 onions, chopped
1 green pepper, seeded and chopped
225 g (8 oz) mushrooms
100 g (4 oz) fresh wholemeal breadcrumbs
2 eggs
sea salt
freshly ground black pepper
1 teaspoon dried mixed herbs

Melt the butter and fry the onions and green pepper until soft. Finely chop half the mushrooms and fry with the pepper and onion. Remove from the heat and add breadcrumbs and eggs. Add the salt, pepper and mixed herbs.

Shape into burgers and grill. Slice and fry the remaining mushrooms and serve on top of the burgers or in rolls.

GARLIC BREAD
Serves 4

1 French loaf
125 g (5 oz) butter
4 teaspoons Herb and Garlic Dip
salt

Make incisions horizontally along the length of the loaf. Blend the butter, Herb and Garlic Dip and salt together. Fill the incisions with this mixture, wrap in foil and bake for 10–20 minutes at 180C (350F, mark 4).

INDEX

air drying, 18
allspice, 20
Almond risotto, spiced, 64
Anchoïade, 50
Apple and fig pie, 82
arrowroot, 20

Banana
    and date chutney, 89
    bread, 86
basil, 20, 21
bay leaves, 21
Béchamel sauce, 88
Beef, 39, 40
    kebabs, barbecued, 57
    and onions, stir-fried, 69
beverages, 40
Biscuits,
    Easter spice, 84
    ginger shortbread, 84
bouquets garnis, 35
Bread, 40
    banana, 86
    garlic, 94
Brochettes de poisson
        provençales, 76
Burgers, mushroom, 94

cakes and biscuits, 40
Cannelloni, 54
caraway seeds, 22, 23
capsicums, 23
cardamom, 23
casseroles and stews, 40
Cauliflower, curried, and
        potato, (Gobi Alu

Masala), 72
celery salt, 35
Chapatis, 73
cheese, 40
    soufflé, 53
Cheese and lentil loaf, 63
Chicken
    baked (Tandoori Murgha),
        70
    cacciatore, 80
    chowder, 49
    crispy, with sweet and sour
        sauce, 66
    French-style, 77
    hotpot, 58
    Tikka, 70
Chick pea casserole, 62
Chilli sauce, red, 90
Chinese dishes, 41
Chinese five spice, 35
chives, 23
Chive and cucumber soup,
        iced, 47
Chutney, date and banana,
        89
chutneys and pickles, 41
cinnamon, 24
cloves, 24
Cod Portuguese, 58
Coleslaw, rainbow, 51
coriander, 24
Courgettes, stuffed, 61
Cucumber and chive soup,
        iced, 47
Cucumber raita, 73
cumin, 25

Curry blends,
    garam masala, 36
    hot madras, 36
    mild madras, 36
    Roghan josh, 36
    tandoori, 35
    vindaloo, 36
curry leaves, 25
    powder, 25

Dal, 74
Date and banana chutney,
        89
dill tops, 25
Dips,
    party, 93
    curry, 37
    French onion, 37
    herb and garlic, 37
    seafood, 37

Easter spice biscuits, 84
Egg foo yung, 69

fennel seed, 25, 26
fenugreek, 26
Fettucine con prosciutto, 55
Fig and apple pie, 82
fines herbes, 36
Fish, 41
    deep-fried spiced, 68
    kebabs, lemon, 92
    skewered, 76
    sliced in wine sauce (Liu
        Yu-Pien), 68

freeze-dried range of spices, 18, 19
freeze drying, 18
French
  cuisine, 74
  dishes, 41
fruit, 42

galangal, 26
garlic, 26
  bread, 94
  grain pepper, 27
  mayonnaise, 89
  salt, 36
Gazpacho Andalusian, 48
Gigot aux abricots, 75
Ginger, 27
  shortbread biscuits, 84
  sponge pudding, 83
Gnocchi di polenta, 80
Gobi Alu Masala, 72

Herb omelette, 76
herbes provençales, 36
herbs, mixed, 37
Hoppin' John, 61

Indian dishes, 42
Italian
  cuisine, 78
  seasoning, 36

juniper berries, 27

Kebabs
  Husaini, 72
  lemon fish, 92
Kipper pâté, 50
Koftas (curried meatballs), 71

Lamb, 42
  apricot stuffed, with
    rosemary, 75
  grilled on skewers (Husaini
    kebabs), 72
  Peking braised, 65
Lasagne al forno, 56
Lemon fish kebabs, 92
lemon grass, 28
Lentil and cheese loaf, 63

mace, 28
marinades, 42, 43
marjoram, 28
Mayonnaise, garlic, 89
Meatballs, curried (Koftas),
    71
mint,
  applemint, 28
  spearmint, 28
Moules marinière, 78
Mulled wine, 92
Mussels in white wine, 78
Mushroom burgers, 94
mustard seed, 29

nutmeg, 28

Omelette,
  aux fines herbes, 76
  Harlequin soufflé, 52
oregano, 29

parsley, 29, 30
Peperoni ripieni, 79
pepper, black, 21, 22
  Boston grain, 22
  Bristol blend five, 22
  green, berries, 27
  Jamaican, 36
  lemon grain, 28
  steak, 37
  white, 34
peppercorns, Sichuan, 32
Peppers, stuffed, 79
Piccalilli, 87
pickling spice, 37
poppy seed, 30
Pork chops, hot sweet, 57
Potato salad, 51
Potatoes, ash-baked plugged,
    93
Poulet à l'Estragon, 77
poultry, 43
puddings, pies, 43

Relish, tomato, 90
Rice, 43, 74
  creamed, with sherry, 83
Risotto, spiced almond, 64

rosemary, 30

salads, 43, 44
salt,
  onion, 37
  sea, 30, 31
saffron, 31
sage, 31
Sauces, 44
  Béchamel, 88
  Red chilli, 90
  Tartare, 89
Sausage and prune stuffing,
    91
seafood, 44
sesame,
  sables, 85
  seeds, 31, 32
Shrimp à la creole, 60
soups, stocks, 44
spice, mixed, 37
Sponge pudding, ginger, 83
star anise, 32
Stir-fried beef and onions, 69
stuffing, 44
sugar, 44
Sweet and sour sauce, with
    crispy chicken, 66

Tandoori Murgha (baked
    chicken), 70
tarragon, 32, 33
Tartare sauce, 90
thyme, 33
Tomato
  relish, 90
  soup, 48
Tuna steaks with potatoes,
    59
turmeric, 33

vanilla pod, 34
Vegetable casserole, 62
vegetables, 44, 45
vegetarian dishes, 45

Wine,
  mulled, 92
  mulling spices, 38